Two-Factor Authentication

Two-Factor Authentication

MARK STANISLAV

IT Governance Publishing

IT Governance Publishing
IT Governance Limited
Unit 3, Clive Court
Bartholomew's Walk
Cambridgeshire Business Park
Ely, Cambridgeshire
CB7 4EA
United Kingdom
www.itgovernance.co.uk

First published in the United Kingdom in 2015
by IT Governance Publishing

ISBN 978-1-84928-732-6

FOREWORD

If there is a more hated, feared, or otherwise misunderstood word associated with information technology than 'password', I don't know it.

My authentication-security baptism occurred in 1982 during my first commercial security project fixing the 30-line password algorithm of ACF2 (SKK, Inc.). Since then, I've only gone further down the rabbit hole of this critical area of information security.

Because ACF2 was the leading mainframe security product, and the primary product protecting US and other Western governments, we were heavily involved with trust certifications. These included C2 and B1 levels of assurance documented in the 'Orange Book' in the noted 'Rainbow Series' from the Department of Defense (DoD).

The 'Green Book' in the series dealt with password controls – this is where the commercial debate began in earnest. We at SKK, Inc. broke rank with our DoD counterparts and officially told our customers that the 'Green Book' controls were more dangerous than helpful for security.

For instance, implementers were told to store the last ten passwords of an account to determine if password reuse was occurring. At the time, we believed that sticky-note sales would skyrocket with such guidance – little did we know just how accurate that prediction was. Against our customers' desires, we refused to budge on this issue and instead decided to act.

We opened our development doors inviting strong-authentication vendors to solve the problem. We introduced a new feature to ACF2/MVS 3.1.5 called Extended User Authentication Exit Facility, a.k.a. EUA Exit. The more notable companies we saw participate were Gordian Systems Inc., Enigma Logic and Security Dynamics. Today, these companies collectively represent the innovators behind many of the core one-time password (OTP) technologies you will read about in this book.

I personally tried my hand with a biometric startup in 1987 called ThumbScan. Our dream could not get out of the lab so we pivoted to 'plan B' and bought the failing Gordian OTP product and patents. ThumbScan/Gordian unfortunately failed as well, but years later I tried again under the Value Added Systems Company (VASCO) flag and finally got it right.

Ken Hunt, the CEO of VASCO, believed that security patents might be 'important someday', and I was still convinced the dreaded password was a scourge to computing. We set off in 1994 to change the world and this time we accomplished our goal by protecting banks across the globe – except for the US. We scratched our heads on that one for years.

Even as products were refined over the years, the industry barely noticed. Sure, some of us were successful but in the grand scheme of things the problems far outpaced solutions – things got worse, not better. Considering that, why *are* passwords so damning still today?

Foremost, the problem isn't the idea of a password but rather that most passwords are created and managed by humans. A computer can generate and store a great password but humans will often create passwords that can be committed to memory. This leads to poor password selection and a high amount of reuse across systems.

Second, the number of accounts being created and maintained has exacerbated the aforementioned problems. We're at a point where a social network for knitting could have its passwords stolen and criminals will drain bank accounts around the US.

Lastly, we have all underestimated pain thresholds – just how bad does it have to get? Our craziest fear-mongering marketers at VASCO couldn't have written the headlines we see today. This last point, I'm afraid to say, is still with us, but a divide is happening where competitive advantages will separate winners and losers along trust lines.

The FIDO (Fast IDentity Online) Alliance – a not-for-profit consortium focused on open standards and interoperability around authentication security – has done a fantastic job in bringing many stakeholders to the table with the stated objective of killing passwords. Does anyone believe passwords will actually be 'killed'? Of course they don't. Can we bring far better solutions collectively to the industry than any one company? Absolutely.

The industry call to action is that application owners become activists. While no one entity can solve this, a class of entities can. It takes an activist, however, to start the ball rolling and two notable FIDO participants are PayPal and Google. When application owners realise that millions of existing end-user devices can be trusted, at no additional cost to either party, things will finally change in this industry.

This is the way forward, and when coupled with advancements in contextual authentication and better open standards, the future looks quite bright. Not just for a single country or industry but for authentication security as a whole.

While I am not surprised, I am sincerely sad, that so many of our predictions from previous decades came true. It tells me that we, the security industry, failed to accomplish what we were tasked to do – protect users.

The good news is that many of us have never given up. We are a persistent bunch and we've welcomed new minds to the fight. I have never been as confident as I am today that everyday technology users will soon have great authentication security choices to protect themselves at scale.

It's been a long, hard-fought battle, but I hope that we're on the cusp of finally taking power away from the bad guys and putting it back in the hands of the end user.

John Haggard
Chief Business Officer, Yubico

PREFACE

Two-factor authentication is an ever-increasing necessity in information technology as the threats facing end-user security become more intense and powerful. As criminals continue to improve their techniques to steal user credentials and otherwise circumvent traditional, single-factor authentication security mechanisms, there's a pressing need for individuals and organisations to understand their options better when it comes to authentication.

It is my experience that much of the thinking regarding two-factor authentication is actually based on decades-old knowledge about how, why and when people should deploy such authentication security. Further, any matter already written about this topic is limited to a few pages of a book on overall information security and not a standalone effort to summarise this topic in a sufficient manner.

This book intends to provide an introduction to the topic of two-factor authentication for those technologists who have yet to be deeply engaged with this important subject matter. Still, even those with previous two-factor authentication experience may not be fully aware of the technologies available, or trends in progress, around the broad subject of authentication security.

The following subject matter will be covered:

- Chapter 1 aims to provide readers with important foundational knowledge to frame the subjects discussed in this book.
- Chapter 2 will address why two-factor authentication is so critical to IT and the concerning reality of password-only security.
- Chapter 3 provides readers with key two-factor authentication basics that are core to many of the discussed technologies throughout this book.
- Chapter 4 covers six key groupings of two-factor authentication technologies with a focus on their strengths, weaknesses and important nuances.
- Chapter 5 conveys international examples of standards and regulations that make two-factor authentication a component of security guidance.
- Chapter 6 details how everyday end-users are interacting with two-factor authentication and provides insight into the drivers behind their use.
- Chapter 7 suggests how two-factor authentication will continue to evolve and where we'll see increased adoption in the future.

My hope is that you, the reader, will gain a sense of understanding of the means with which you can not only protect your own accounts and technologies, but also help influence the decisions of the organisations you work with and for.

ABOUT THE AUTHOR

Mark Stanislav is an information technology professional with over a decade of varied experience in systems administration, web application development and information security. Mark is currently a Senior Security Consultant for the Strategic Services team at Rapid7.

Mark has spoken internationally at nearly 100 events including RSA, DEF CON, SecTor, SOURCE Boston, ShmooCon, and THOTCON. News outlets such as the *Wall Street Journal*, *Al Jazeera America*, *Fox Business*, *MarketWatch*, *CNN Money*, *Yahoo Finance*, *Marketplace* and *The Register* have featured Mark's research, initiatives and insights on information security.

Mark earned both his Bachelor of Science degree in networking & IT administration and his Master of Science degree in technology studies, focused on information assurance, from Eastern Michigan University. He also holds CISSP, Security+, Linux+, and CCSK certifications.

xii

ACKNOWLEDGEMENTS

To my wife, Sarah, for her constant love, support and patience as I pursue entirely too many projects at the same time. You're the best and I love you dearly.

To my parents, Ivan and Mary, for believing that I could achieve great things, regardless of how many times I broke our home computer growing up. Your support has meant everything. I love you both.

To my brother, Scott, my sister-in-law, Tara, and my amazing nephews, Nathan and Foster, for being such a wonderful and caring part of my life.

To my in-laws, Barbara, Jim and Derek, thank you for welcoming me into your family so warmly.

To my friends, James Turner and Matt Fanto, thanks for the insight and companionship you've provided over the years to help me grow in IT and beyond.

To my personal book editors, Thu Pham and Zach Lanier, thank you for your time, expertise and friendship. I hope the steak dinner was worth it. Thanks also to Antonio Velasco, CEO of Sinersys Technologies, ir. H.L. (Maarten) Souw RE, Enterprise Risk and QA Manager, UVW and Phil Benn, Principal Information Security Consultant, 24 Security for their helpful comments during the review process.

To Vicki Utting, Joe Pettit and Sally Lanier, thanks for believing in me and making this book a reality.

CONTENTS

CHAPTER 1: INTRODUCTION

Everything old is new again

Existing information-security technologies and processes often resemble historical methods to provide confidentiality, integrity and availability.

In the Middle Ages, the use of castle walls, gates, and drawbridges allowed for certain people to come or go only as desired by those in charge. Today, a firewall ensures that data can only enter or leave specific network ports as defined by configured filtering-rule sets. Similarly, Julius Caesar utilised primitive cryptography thousands of years ago to transmit instructions and guidance to his Roman army. While cryptography still has its place among military engagements, it also helps us protect everything from our private photos to credit card numbers for online shopping.

Authentication is no different, with a rich history of methods proving that you are who you say you are before certain privilege or authorisation is granted.

If you've ever seen a signet ring, you may have been intrigued that it could provide a means to ensure that a document was sealed by a certain party whose ring symbol you knew of. What if you received a letter from a person that was sealed with a signet ring and then met them in person? Would presenting their ring as proof of identity satisfy you? What if the letter they had sealed included information about a scar on their face and a code word they'd say to you upon first meeting?

Within authentication security, the method to prove identity breaks down into three 'factor classes', each with their own pros and cons. The previous example involving the signet ring and letter actually encompasses all three of the factor classes rather succinctly.

1 **The signet ring** represents 'what you have'.
2 **The facial scar** represents 'what you are'.
3 **The code word** represents 'what you know'.

Today, authentication factor classes are better represented by a slightly more tech-forward list:

1 **A smartphone** represents 'what you have'.
2 **A fingerprint** represents 'what you are'.
3 **A password** represents 'what you know'.

The capabilities afforded to us by modern technology provide a wealth of means to handle our existing factor classes in new ways. As you'll read, this opens up exciting possibilities for authentication security as we've known it for decades.

You've been using two-factor for years

For the majority of people worldwide, passwords and personal identification numbers (PINs) are how users authenticate themselves to systems and services in their daily lives. These values are representative of the 'what you know' factor class. Much like a predetermined code word, a password is really an agreement between a system and a user that, each time they 'meet', the password will validate that the user coming back to the system is who they claim to be.

However, if you've used an ATM or bought something with a debit card, you've actually engaged in using two-factor authentication. By possessing the debit card (what you have) and typing a PIN (what you know), you've utilised two factor classes for one authentication process.

Mixing factor classes leads to better security because it's unlikely that a criminal could compromise both authentication mechanisms. Imagine if someone stole your wallet at a bar one night. They may now have your debit card (something you had), but without the PIN (something you know) they are unable to withdraw funds. If, one day, someone saw your PIN over your shoulder as you entered it into an ATM, they may know that value but still not have the card they need to present to the machine.

Since the ATM security we know today was patented back in the 1960s, it would seem reckless if the banking industry took away one of those factors of authentication to access your financial accounts. Amazingly, though, the majority of people who have used online banking for decades still wield only a password as their means to achieve the same goal.

Many of the technologies we use today (like online banking), have grown organically as capabilities to provide advanced functions to customers have become more realistic. Indeed, 15 years ago there were few cheap, reliable, easy-to-use and efficient means for two-factor authentication to be added to everyone's online banking experiences. As a result, we're now seeing financial institutions play catch-up in the digital world to gain parity with their physical banking counterparts.

Authentication security's naming problem

One of the biggest issues with authentication security is the inability of the industry to name the technology clearly and concisely. Further, even well informed technologists and companies quite often use authentication security terms incorrectly, leading to unnecessary confusion. This point is well noted by the usage of so-called 'security images'.

Security images are really a staple of the online financial industry's attempt to provide additional protection to customer accounts without frustrating their users. Typically, a customer will select an image from a list of perhaps twenty that will be shown to them upon logging into their account. The usage of that image, however, is often conflated with the wrong type of security focus.

A security image can actually provide a benefit to customers by appearing when they are prompted to type their username and password into a site. If a user doesn't see their specific image shown, they can be implicitly warned that a criminal may be attempting to steal their credentials through the usage of a fraudulent website. Unfortunately, this security benefit is often used incorrectly by treating it as a 'second factor', which it most certainly is not.

Remember, two-factor authentication requires two different factor classes to be used for one authentication transaction. A password is something the banking customer knows – and so is the security image. As a phishing-mitigation technique, security images may suffice, but do not accomplish the goals of two-factor authentication. While two steps from the same factor class isn't necessarily bad, it's not as secure as using two factor classes.

This leads us into the other aspect of naming that goes sideways for people: 'I thought two-factor authentication was called [insert phrase or acronym] instead!' Here's a quick breakdown:

- **Two-factor authentication:** use of two factor classes to provide authentication. This is also represented as '2FA' and 'TFA'.
- **Multi-factor authentication:** use of two or more factor classes to provide authentication. This is also represented as 'MFA'.
- **Two-step verification:** use of two independent steps for authentication that might not involve two separate factor classes. This is also represented as '2SV'.
- **Strong authentication:** authentication beyond simply a password. May be represented by the usage of 'security questions', or could be layered security like two-factor authentication.

Factor classes, when used together, are often referred to as primary and secondary methods of authentication. This book will typically discuss the secondary form of authentication used and implies that a password or PIN is the primary method. While certain facilities, government agencies or even corporations may not use a 'what-you-know' factor in their authentication process, most readers will likely do just that for the foreseeable future.

Looking down a road to greater adoption

I would suspect that many readers of this book have been using computing technologies for perhaps decades and likely had little to no interaction with two-factor authentication up to this point. The reason for this could vary wildly, but one reason is that unless your employers made you use it, few people would ever think that they could or should use such a level of authentication security for their day-to-day activities. Part of this reasoning goes to the fact that, until rather recently, the cost and complexity of deploying and using methods in this technology space were very prohibitive for most people's lives.

Technologies best known to existing users of two-factor authentication will likely be hardware-based. That's to say, their second factor would be 'what you have', such as a hardware token that would generate a one-time password (OTP) value. These devices typically range between US$25 and US$100, and for a business that you were a customer of, it's unlikely they would just give them out to everyone (for free, anyway). Further, even if your financial institution or stock-trading company offered you one, you may have been annoyed at the prospect of having to carry a device on your keyring or in your wallet to log in online.

These two points (cost and end-user frustration) have unfortunately been traits of authentication security for decades. This isn't to say that successful authentication vendors were doing anything wrong, simply that technology was not yet at the level necessary to reduce the costs and complexity associated with making security applicable for most users' needs. Could you imagine the effort and cost of supplying the millions of customers of a multinational bank with hardware tokens? Taking on the overheads of purchasing, shipping, managing and supporting such an effort would be extremely unwise.

The road to adoption, while slow overall, has sped up within just the past decade due to technologies such as Cloud computing and smartphones, relieving much of the cost and complexity of widely deploying and managing a proper two-factor authentication solution. The addition of open standards for OTP generation has allowed vendors to build hardware that works on any number of platforms, helping to reduce cost and create more incentive for organisations to make the investment to buy devices they can use with a number of vendors.

As you learn more about the technologies, standards, risks and use cases of two-factor authentication throughout this book, be mindful to figure out what will work best for *your* needs. There are a wide variety of vendors, methods and implementation styles available to complement the specific goals that you or your organisation have.

CHAPTER 2: RISKS TO ONE-FACTOR AUTHENTICATION

Our solutions are also our problems

Depending on your level of computing technology experience, you may be more or less familiar with three major models in architecture:

1 Mainframe computing
2 Client–server computing
3 Cloud-mobile computing

Each of these models represents a fundamental shift in the way computing architects leverage resources (memory, storage, processing power, etc.) and how those resources are made available to end-users.

In mainframe computing, the resources were highly centralised, with perhaps a couple of large machines that would allow many users to access them and share resources. A client–server model, however, shifted much of the computing resources and effort down to individual workstations for users, while offsetting server needs down to a minimal amount – usually focused on data storage and file sharing. Lastly, and most recently, the era of Cloud-mobile has decentralised computing to the point where a service may be entirely separate from the architecture of the business using it. Today, the Cloud-mobile era that allows the two-factor authentication market to prosper has also made the need for such authentication all the more real.

Networks in mainframe and client–server models were often tied to private and highly restricted networks that afforded a sense of security to the data and services behind firewalls and intrusion prevention systems. Similar to the castle walls we spoke of previously, these older models of computing architecture were predicated on keeping bad people out and good data in. However, once an attacker breaks through these walls, many of these networks are soft and malleable to those wishing to do harm. This reality is even more concerning when you consider organisations are moving their data, processing power and even their email into 'the Cloud'.

Companies like Google and Salesforce.com are stunning examples of how meaningful Cloud computing can be for big businesses, universities, and other entities that want to solve large-scale problems, but not take on the responsibility of managing their own servers, data centres and software updates. It also shouldn't come as a shock that both of these companies offer two-factor authentication to protect sensitive data from criminals who wish to steal it.

Attacking password-only security

On 18 December 2013, journalist Brian Krebs released information on his website that stated that retailer Target had been breached. As details eventually came out about how this attack was executed, it came to light that stolen credentials (a username and password) from a heating, cooling and ventilation (HVAC) contractor were used as the first real foothold in Target's network. This is, of course, not the first or the last story like this, but it does show an important point: authentication security matters.

2: Risks to One-Factor Authentication

In the case of Target, the HVAC contractor had been compromised through a phishing attack that used malware to steal the aforementioned credentials. Whether those credentials logged the contractor into a virtual private network (VPN), a Target portal, or any other system or network, that leap of authorisation is often enough for a skilled attacker to make their next move.

A few of the ways that attackers break into networks and systems protected only by single-factor authentication are:

- **Phishing:** sending out an email that requests a user to perform an action, such as change their password. The site a victim types the password into is usually under the control of the attacker.
- **Malware:** software that performs nefarious actions against the device it's installed on. Often used as a key-logger to retrieve credentials typed into web-based logins by the victim.
- **Brute force:** attackers try to guess a victim's password by testing the most commonly used passwords and even generating character combinations.
- **Hash cracking:** stolen databases often have cryptographically protected passwords that in many cases can be 'cracked' to reveal the user's actual password. These passwords would then be used in attempts to log into victim accounts.
- **Physical:** passwords written on sticky notes or observed as the victim types it into their machine.
- **Retrieval:** an attacker answering security questions can often retrieve a password when it's stored in plain text or a reversible format.

These methods clearly reduce the security benefits that passwords are supposed to offer. Taking that into consideration, it's not hard to believe that even large companies such as Target can be breached. The foothold required to lead attackers to a treasure trove of credit card details in one of the largest breaches in history all started with a single password from a person not even employed directly by the company. This is where single-factor security quickly shows what's at stake and why practitioners need to do better.

The 'fix' isn't just better passwords

Often when security experts discuss single-factor authentication, the contention quickly becomes, 'If we just used better passwords, there'd be no need for two-factor authentication!' The logic behind that statement is that if eight-character passwords get brute-forced, let's make them 14 characters instead. Similarly, if passwords are dictionary words, let's force complexity rules to make users create passwords that will take a long time to crack. The problem is that this whack-a-mole approach leaves users frustrated and organisations with little benefit in exchange for a lot of extra training and oversight.

Phishing attacks, for instance, are both easily executed and quite beneficial to attackers in terms of results for effort spent. Password-complexity rules and length literally do *nothing* to stop a phishing campaign from succeeding. Due to the prevalence of phishing and the obvious benefit (remember, that's how Target's breach started), attackers rarely have any need to brute-force or crack passwords unless other means have failed. This is a great example of how a typical, 'if it's leaking, add more sandbags' approach in information security doesn't apply to passwords.

Further, malware that steals passwords from users' computers is easily capable of recording the keystrokes typed into a website or just intercepting the entire conversation in the first place. Passwords aren't themselves capable of deciding whether or not a login attempt looks fraudulent. Passwords are also not able to say, 'Don't let this transaction happen, the person who typed it in isn't who they say they are!'

What's truly concerning is that phishing and malware are not new techniques and are only increasing in usage and, inherently, effectiveness. Conflating the use of Cloud services with the weakness of passwords yields great results for attackers and a lot of rational concern for organisations and individuals.

Notably, the malware called 'Dyre' targets Salesforce.com users by attempting to trick them into entering their credentials into a malicious clone of the intended website. This helps attackers gain the precious login details of people who may have access to much of the financial data of a company. At this point, an attacker has all they need in most circumstances to breach an organisation, steal data and then either sell that valuable data or attempt to extort the target. No password-complexity rule would prevent this type of attack.

The unfortunate reality is that while passwords in their current form were 'good enough' in early computing, they've hung on entirely too long as the only means to protect the mounds of sensitive data we store and communications we engage in.

CHAPTER 3: UNDERSTANDING THE BASICS

In-band and out-of-band authentication

To understand the current options on the market for two-factor authentication, two key concepts are in-band and out-of-band methods. The choice of how to authenticate is more than just the mechanism (e.g. hardware, software, etc.) but also the medium used to transmit authentication data.

When using a device like a hardware token that generates a one-time password, that value is likely sent through the same transmission channel of authentication as your primary credentials. Imagine, for instance, if you were to log into a web-based email account with your username and password. As part of the authentication process, you would also have to transmit the generated OTP value for your second factor of authentication. This represents in-band two-factor authentication.

In our scenario, if an attacker is able to steal your username and password, they are also likely to be able to steal the OTP value. This can render the addition of two-factor authentication somewhat moot depending on the control they can exhibit over your authentication process. While the ability for an attacker to carry out such an attack isn't trivial in many cases, the use of malware is a great example in which this type of attack can succeed easily.

Many users of the gaming company Blizzard were impacted by a well-disguised malware that intercepted not only their primary credentials, but also their generated OTP value used for secondary authentication. By doing this, criminals were able to compromise gamers' accounts and steal their digital wares for profit. This is a perfect example of where an end-user was trying to protect their account through two-factor authentication but ultimately let their personal machine be compromised, thus allowing an attacker to exert control over their authentication process.

Out-of-band authentication, conversely, separates the channels of authentication such that even if your primary credentials are stolen, an attacker can't easily capture the second factor. This has the obvious advantage of requiring an attacker to go to much greater lengths to thwart the additional security provided by the second factor.

If your bank, for instance, calls your mobile phone after you try to log into your online account, this is an example of an out-of-band second factor of authentication. A criminal may be able to control your computer, but unless they've also stolen your mobile phone or hijacked your call forwarding, they are not able to influence the authentication process in this scenario.

As you evaluate methods to perform two-factor authentication, consider the risk and convenience of each, including the important nuance of in-band versus out-of-band when deciding what makes sense for your specific organisational or personal needs.

Generating one-time passwords

One recurring topic of two-factor authentication, historically and now, is the ability for a device or piece of software to generate a one-time password. The ability to create a number based on a strict set of criteria that both the client (device/software) and the confirming server can agree upon – but which a nefarious third party can't guess – is the strength of OTP generation.

Each method of OTP generation we will discuss requires the use of a secret. Both the client generating an OTP and the server that verifies it know this secret. By using this secret value in conjunction with the rest of an applicable OTP-generation algorithm, the actual secret is never transmitted through an authentication transaction, but rather the algorithm has utilised it to create the OTP displayed. This prevents an attacker from being able to generate their own valid OTP results, even if they are able to steal an OTP while it's being transmitted.

Generating a one-time password implies that if someone steals an OTP value from a user and tries to use it, that value will only work if it has not been used to authenticate previously. Due to this, it's important for the server handling authentication to keep track of which OTP values are actually used during the window when the code is valid.

The methods to generate this OTP vary, but we will cover a few of the major types of this process and related algorithms.

(a) Event-based

An event-based algorithm typically ties the one-time password-generation process to an incremented value. If a token generated an OTP from a counter value of 126, for instance, the server would only match that OTP if its own counter had the same number. An end-user may press a button to generate the next OTP, and when that's successfully sent to the server, the number is incremented.

Since synchronisation is done through the authentication process, a user who happens to press their token's OTP-generation button a few times without any authentication attempt can break the aforementioned synchronisation quite easily. If the client and server are out of sync, the synchronisation must be re-established by an administrator for continued use of that OTP device.

Notably, an algorithm that's event-based can be abused if an attacker is able to steal an OTP code and use it to access an end-user's account before the end-user does. Since codes are based on an incremented value, the validating server won't have any ability to know whether a code is one second or 20 hours old.

The hash-based one-time-password (HOTP) algorithm of the Initiative for Open Authentication (OATH), which became a standard in 2005, is an example of event-based OTP generation. Many hardware- and software-based tokens from organisations such as Swivel, Yubico and SurePassID utilise the HOTP algorithm since it's an open standard.

Between concern about synchronisation issues and the possibility of an attacker abusing the potentially long life of event-based OTP algorithms, this style of OTP generation is fading in popularity relative to its contemporaries.

(b) Time-based

Time-based algorithms leverage a clock as part of the OTP generation. If both the client and server's time are relatively in sync with one another, this algorithm is able to generate an OTP that will match on both sides. This method has a direct advantage over event-based algorithms in that the synchronisation doesn't rely on a number to be incremented, thereby decreasing the likelihood of out-of-sync issues. Clock synchronisation doesn't change based on the number of attempts, but rather provides a window in which a given OTP is valid.

Time-based OTPs are typically only valid for 30 to 60 seconds, which is ideal for security. This dramatically limits the timeframe in which an attacker could leverage a stolen OTP value. This is in stark contrast to the long-life OTP values that pose a security risk with event-based algorithms like HOTP.

Examples of authentication solutions that use time-based algorithms are RSA's SecurID and OATH's time-based one-time-password algorithm, otherwise known as TOTP (RFC 6238). Modern hardware and software tokens are likely to use TOTP to provide OTP generation due to their benefits of a reduced attack surface and reduced maintenance of synchronisation between client and server.

It's important to note that, like event-based OTP, time-based algorithms still require the server to keep track of values used in order to avoid replaying a single OTP within the valid window by an attacker. This subtlety is often forgotten during the implementation of algorithms like TOTP.

(c) Challenge response

One-time password generation that requires a user's input of a 'challenge' into the device before an OTP is presented is known as challenge-response. The 'challenge' could be a word or a PIN the user will be shown during their authentication process that is utilised in the OTP-generation algorithm.

In the case of the OATH Challenge-Response Algorithm, known as OCRA (RFC 6287), OATH is built on top of HOTP and added to the challenge component to determine what OTP value to generate. While OCRA doesn't specify that you must utilise time or other session-related information, you are able to do so if so desired based on the standard.

The extra process of showing a user a challenge value and requiring them to type that into their hardware may hinder authentication workflows. While challenge-response has been around for many years, OCRA has only existed since mid-2011 and is not widely implemented compared with other OATH algorithms. Example authentication solution implementations of challenge-response are VASCO's DIGIPASS 260, FEITIAN's OTP c300, and Yubico's Yubikey.

CHAPTER 4: SECOND-FACTOR TECHNOLOGIES

A burgeoning world of options

If you were to ask a number of reasonably well informed security professionals, "What is two-factor authentication?" you'd likely get a consistent answer: "Hardware tokens that generate random numbers." This view isn't unfair or inaccurate in the macro view of the world since it's been 30 years since Kenneth Weiss filed his patent for what would become the very well known RSA SecurID token. This single line of devices has propelled the RSA brand into the pockets of many of the most important professionals over the past few decades, and was, in many ways, one of the few options of computer-focused two-factor authentication security in a typical enterprise.

Today, two-factor authentication is a much larger playing field and has gone beyond smartcards and hardware tokens. In this chapter, we will summarise many of the most popular methods of two-factor authentication used today and explain the upsides and downsides to each type of technology. By the end of this chapter, you should have a clearer picture of what options you have for your own authentication security needs and how this world is moving quickly with regard to two-factor authentication security.

Hardware-based OTP generation

It seems fitting to begin with the quintessential method of performing two-factor authentication in place across the enterprise for decades now. Hardware tokens generating a one-time password are iconic, with their attachment to the keyrings of millions of professionals internationally. If you've been a corporate user of two-factor authentication prior to 2010, you've likely done so with one of these devices.

As previously conveyed, the algorithm handling OTP generation can vary device to device, but so can the form factor of the actual hardware. Whether the OTP is shown on a screen, transmitted via USB, or even sent over Bluetooth to a user's workstation wirelessly, the mechanism still requires a device to properly generate an accurate and synchronised OTP value.

Hardware-token interaction is dependent on the method of OTP used. Time-based OTP tokens will simply display a new number every 30 to 60 seconds. If the token is using an event-based algorithm, they will likely have a button to press to generate a new value. Lastly, if the token is challenge-response-based, the user will be given a 'challenge' value which must be entered into the device and the resulting output will be their OTP value.

After the value is displayed, users must read and type the value into the relevant two-factor-enabled website or application for processing alongside their primary credentials.

Hardware tokens typically last up to five years in most form factors but the opportunity to lose or break the device during that window may accelerate the need to replace the unit.

Arguably, the best-known hardware OTP token would be the RSA SecurID, which leverages a proprietary time-based OTP algorithm. This device has evolved lightly over the past couple of decades, with the SID-700 model being what many people think of when they are discussing what two-factor authentication is and 'looks like'.

While the SecurID algorithm is proprietary to RSA, the generation process is reasonably well understood at this point. An open-source software project called *stoken* exists that is capable of generating OTP values compatible with many implementations of RSA's hardware and software. Still, compared to standards such as HOTP and TOTP, RSA's SecurID is a bit of an anomaly these days with many vendors moving to OATH standards, including offerings such as SafeNet's SafeWord, Fortinet's FortiToken, and VASCO's DIGIPASS GO 6.

Other form factors using the same underlying technology do exist, including a device that is the size of a credit card. The keyring hardware token, while small, can often make a keyring bulky and annoy its user. Further, many people who work from a single location may just leave the device sitting on their desk for easier use. While this scenario isn't ideal from a security perspective – the device is meant to stay with its user – there's still much more security than if a user were only using a password.

For many implementations of hardware tokens, each user is only provisioned a single device, which limits their ability to log in if they make a long commute home and then realise they can't log into their company's VPN. PayPal, for instance, changed from providing keyring-style tokens to credit card-sized devices for their 'Security Key' in 2010.

While not a foolproof solution to the problem of leaving an OTP-generating device behind at work, the ability to store this unit in your wallet lends itself to being easier to transport and reduces the likelihood that you may forget it. The theme of convenient security is a cornerstone of two-factor authentication adoption (or lack thereof).

Due to the influx of mobile devices, especially smartphones and tablets, the usefulness of a separate hardware token has been slipping in the past few years. Some companies, such as VASCO, have been trying to elegantly blur the line between mobile operation and hardware-token technology. With the DIGIPASS GO 215, VASCO allows users to leverage a Bluetooth-enabled hardware token to transmit its OTP value to a mobile device's applications. While this device is a clever implementation of new technology paired with old, the use of standalone hardware tokens has few benefits compared to what modern mobile devices are capable of.

Another exciting up-and-coming brand in the authentication space is Yubico, whose Yubikey line of devices is starting to permeate organisations large and small. With a USB form factor ranging from a small dongle to a fingertip-sized version, Yubico provides an open ecosystem to their hardware, giving people the control they've never had before with such hardware OTP devices. Yubico provides a free utility that allows a device owner to configure which types of OTP can be accomplished with a given device and generate new secret key (seed) values as desired.

Unlike many other hardware OTP devices, Yubikey effectively acts as a keyboard when plugged into your machine, allowing it to enter the value for you with no screen reading required. The lack of a screen or battery helps to keep the device line extremely small. The typical usage of Yubikey devices is to simply touch a small pad that initiates the OTP-generation process and sends the resulting string through the USB to the authentication interface. The capability of plugging the device into your laptop or workstation reduces the risk that you'll forget the device when you need it.

Yubikey has also moved into the near-field communication (NFC) space to allow the device to authenticate without requiring insertion into a USB slot. This ends up producing an experience similar to the aforementioned Bluetooth-enabled hardware token from VASCO.

Hardware tokens for OTP generation have a few defining characteristics that explain why they've lasted for decades, and why they're considered the primary method to carry out authentication security processes. Foremost, since these devices perform a single discreet task very well, they aren't a target for malware, viruses or other security impediments that plague typical general computing devices. Further, by requiring no external power source and minimal, if any, maintenance, self-contained OTP-generating hardware has proven easy to deal with from a pure technical standpoint for end-users of the technology.

Another valuable aspect of these devices is the extremely low learning curve for end-users. A user may have to type in a challenge before receiving their OTP value, but in most cases they simply have to type the numbers they see on the screen when prompted during authentication. This benefit is, of course, a key reason why OTP succeeds quite well in the market, regardless of whether its implementation is via hardware or software.

Due to their form factor, hardware OTP devices aren't usually 'fixed' if they have issues. Instead, they have to be replaced by the manufacturer. Related to this, if a criminal steals the unique seed value used in OTP generation, then they're able to generate values, rendering your device useless. The original device would need to be disabled and discarded effectively for security purposes. RSA's SecurID, unfortunately, is a great example of this implicit lack of malleability in most hardware OTP devices.

In 2011, it was confirmed by RSA that they had suffered a security breach of their corporate network. As a result, they eventually offered to replace customers' hardware tokens in order to reduce the potential security impact to customer organisations. The rationale behind such a replacement programme stems from the reports that seed files were stolen during the breach, for at least some customers. If true, the seed values contained in those files could allow a criminal to effectively 'clone' a SecurID token and thus perform second-factor authentication if they also possessed a stolen set of credentials for their target.

In best practice, once a vendor provides a seed file for a token order to a customer, they should delete their information about those seeds to prevent a scenario like this from occurring. However, customers often lose data, and if the vendor doesn't have a backup of the seed file, there's going to need to be a replacement of tokens that someone will ultimately have to pay for.

As we continue to discuss other methods of two-factor authentication popular today, keep in mind that hardware tokens have reliability, ease of use, reduced attack surface and history on their side. While the technology available today eclipses what standard keyring, credit card or other form-factor hardware has been doing for 30 years, they are still a favourite among many end-users for the same reasons they succeeded decades ago.

SMS-based OTP delivery

While hardware tokens in their various forms are an extra item to carry, remember, protect and purchase, Short Message Service (SMS) is able to accomplish a similar goal with a user's existing mobile phone. As of 2010, it was estimated that 6.1 trillion SMS transmissions – colloquially known as 'text' – were sent. Within that immense number were likely a chunk (albeit minuscule) of one-time passwords being delivered to end-users around the world.

While SMS technology goes back to the early 1980s, it's apparent that the early 2000s and beyond have shown tremendous growth in their usage. Notably, mobile phones have been SMS-aware for decades now. That ubiquity and longevity allows even so-called 'feature phones' to provide a means to achieve two-factor authentication without touchscreens and complex mobile applications.

Perhaps surprisingly, the smartphone market only recently surpassed the 'feature phone' market in sales across the world, at the end of 2013. Consider, for a moment, that in 2013 there were roughly 1.8 billion mobile phones sold, and imagine that each one of those is likely capable of performing SMS activities. In context, this means that just about every computing end-user in the world likely has a mobile phone that could be put to worthy use as a mostly free two-factor authentication method.

While the cost to receive an SMS varies widely across the world, there's a good chance that many people either have unlimited SMS with their existing plan, or pay as little as US$5 per month to receive such a service. When people pay per SMS they send or receive, the cost could be a few cents. Either way, the convenience and availability of SMS, combined with the low cost of use, makes this an easy decision for many organisations to provide two-factor authentication to end-users.

Digital telephony providers such as Twilio make it affordable for organisations to send out many SMS messages for a reasonably small amount of money. At around US$0.0075 per message, Twilio would allow an end-user to perform two-factor authentication three times a day, each day of the week, for less than US$1 per month total. When compared to hardware tokens that may be lost, stolen or broken, or just never used, a per-SMS cost seems like a pretty good deal for low-volume usage.

This low cost and ease of use isn't without risk, unfortunately. The same in-band authentication security risks that plague usage of hardware tokens also apply to SMS-based OTP implementations. Further, because mobile phones are often targets of clever malware, the OTP values themselves have grown to be a sought-after target for criminals.

Similar to a typical computer, mobile phones can be compromised a myriad of ways, including through software downloads intended to infect the device, or even through wireless attacks via Bluetooth or cellular communication. From research conducted in 2012 by Dr Jon Oberheide of Duo Security, it was determined that over half of all Android devices contained unpatched vulnerabilities. Each of these issues could be a means with which to compromise a device and ultimately steal sensitive data such as SMS messages.

A notable piece of mobile malware called Eurograbber (a variant of the Zitmo Trojan) stole an estimated €36 million from 30,000 accounts over a few months in 2012. Simply put, Eurograbber steals the contents of a user's mobile device that contains the transaction authorisation number (TAN), which, for our purposes, is the same as an OTP. Once the criminal has this value, they can complete their theft of a victim's bank account with the stolen credentials that they already possess.

While an attacker using Eurograbber is still exerting much more effort than it takes for a person *not* using two-factor authentication to steal money, it cannot be denied that this sort of SMS-centric malware poses a huge risk to OTP delivery in this manner. Moreover, Trojans of this type aren't just for Android but also exist on other mobile platforms, such as BlackBerry.

In most cases, a 'feature phone' is more resilient against malware attacks of this sort due to their simpler, less open platform for custom application installation. Similarly, since Apple's iOS platform restricts the types of application that can be installed on the device, a user would likely have to reduce their phone's built-in security controls in order for it to be vulnerable to an infection by a Trojan. This risk is an ongoing concern for anyone implementing or using SMS-based second-factor technologies.

Applications implementing SMS messaging for the purpose of two-factor authentication are able to do so with less variability in comparison with a typical OTP-generation process like TOTP on a hardware token. The value generated is processed server-side and then simply sent via SMS. The recipient must then type that value during their authentication process. Since the recipient's device is simply a transport, a lack of synchronisation of time won't hinder its effectiveness as an authentication device.

Each time a user properly authenticates their primary credentials the service should generate a new OTP value and transmit it via SMS to the user. If the value does not change after a failed attempt, there's a chance that a criminal could brute-force the value and still log in by guessing it. Further, there should be a limit on the number of second-factor attempts allowed in order to prevent SMS fees from being racked up by an attacker, or an end-user having trouble with the authentication process.

Additionally, if a service does a poor job at generating their OTP values by not using a proper algorithm, they could be rendering their second factor of authentication moot. If the OTP-generating software is flawed in such a way that there are a limited number of possible values created, a clever attack may have better chances of predicting an OTP value.

For instance, if an OTP-generation algorithm uses a combination of the time and a user's unique identification number to create an OTP for each login, an attacker would likely be able to readily create a proper code to bypass the second factor. Thus it is crucial that, as in HOTP and TOTP, randomness play a role in the generation of the values being sent via SMS.

Phone-call-based mechanisms

In a broader manner than even SMS, phone networks are easily able to act as a method of second-factor authentication. Whether you use a mobile phone, voice-over-Internet protocol (VoIP) or a standard home telephone line, interaction with a person via their phone number enables a few different implementations of second-factor validation.

Other than ATM usage, one of the most familiar contexts of two-factor authentication for the everyday person is likely related to financial organisations. If you've ever requested to perform an action on your financial account via the Internet or other means, you may be required to answer a phone call on your registered number to confirm you are who you say you are.

Once the call comes in, you might have to enter the PIN associated with your account or confirm the last four digits of your social security number. By both receiving the call (what you have) and entering your PIN (what you know) you've achieved two-factor authentication via a phone call. This validation process is very simple for telephone users of all technical abilities and ages, but still achieves an important level of validation.

Alternatively, a call may come to your phone and require you to simply press a certain button to validate that a human picked up the call and not an answering machine. Even without the aspect of 'what you know', this process still provides some level of validation that a call was received from a registered phone number, and that the person answering followed directions to complete a request.

In many implementations of phone-call authentication, a user likely completed their first factor via a web application form. Then, they would have been promoted to receive a phone call to satisfy the second factor. In this context, users are actually performing out-of-band second-factor authentication. Since the first factor is via a web form and the second factor occurs via the phone, an attacker wouldn't likely be able to compromise both channels of authentication. This provides a safer process overall.

A phone call could also prompt a user to enter their PIN. A correct entry would prompt the system to read off a one-time password or other value back to the user. The user would then have to type the value into a web form. The flexibility of telephone systems allows many creative methods to achieve a variety of goals based on the security challenges facing an organisation

While SMS is reasonably cheap, telephone calls are even more so. VoIP and other digital providers often have unlimited local and long-distance calling services, meaning that phone authentication methods have a very small financial impact. Further, the telephone system is understood by many people and is not as scary or new as mobile applications or even SMS.

For organisations looking to get a two-factor authentication initiative off the ground or provide it to their customers, phone calls are a great way to satisfy the need without having to put up with much in the way of overheads, training or confusion. Many companies, including Google, Namecheap, Kickstarter and Microsoft enable their users to perform authentication tasks through phone-based means.

Even with the world's broad knowledge of telephone usage, there are a number of risks to using such technology for authentication. For example, a useful feature like call forwarding could pose a risk to phone authentication if a clever attacker successfully reroutes your number to one that they control. Many digital systems, especially those in office networks or VoIP, are easily manipulated with appropriate access. A user may also never be aware that someone temporarily forwarded his or her phone number.

In 2014, Security researcher Shubham Shah found that he was able to bypass numerous two-factor authentication implementations that leveraged phone calls providing users a one-time password. Shah was able to carry out what amounts to phone-number spoofing by recording the automated system's OTP value onto voicemail, which gave him access without actually using the person's phone. While this 'trick' doesn't apply to all networks or carriers, many voicemail systems do not require a PIN to log in, and therefore such a scenario may indeed work.

Telephone calls are also rather disruptive in many ways. Imagine trying to log into your email protected by two-factor authentication while in a quiet business meeting. Even a sly user would still likely make noise trying to get out their phone, answer the call, hear the instructions, press buttons and then put their phone away. At scale, say a few times a day or more, this process becomes rather clunky and slow.

Still, risks and usability concerns aside, phone-based mechanisms are an easy way to achieve authentication security with great flexibility, as they are simple to implement and easy to understand.

Geolocation-aware authentication

Just a few years ago, the idea of having anyone track you constantly was only a worry for the most paranoid among us. Today, we are gladly giving our near-exact geolocation data to a broad set of organisations in exchange for the added convenience in our daily lives of finding new restaurants and telling friends where we are hanging out. More importantly, this geolocation data from phones, tablets, laptops and wearable computers can act as a source of 'truth' to verify that our authentication process is valid.

By creating what's known as a 'geofence' – that is, a perimeter of geographic coordinates – authentication security and less noble services can use the location of our devices to make contextual decisions. For instance, a shopping application on your mobile phone could display a coupon when you enter a retail outlet. While this trivial usage of location data is helpful to a consumer, it's actually rather humble compared to what's actually possible when using geolocation for more sophisticated purposes.

For authentication, users can configure geofence locations – such as their home or office – that will be considered trusted. Upon authentication of primary credentials, location data can be sent to determine whether or not the authenticating user has whitelisted that location as trusted. If they have, they may be logged into the service. If they haven't, they are likely going to have to complete an additional step of authentication to proceed.

Geolocation data isn't an inherently secure means of providing authentication because coordinates can be guessed if you know details about the identity you are trying to impersonate. To provide this security, the geolocation data being sent is likely 'signed' through asymmetric cryptography to state that the data has been generated by a trusted device. It's this step that gives integrity to the data being sent from a device that only the owner should possess.

If you imagine a criminal stealing passwords, they may live in a different country than the person they are attempting to impersonate. As such, when a criminal gets to the second factor of authentication, the geolocation data sent (if there is any) won't match the trusted locations for that user, and will thus require further effort on the attacker's part. If it were the valid user, however, they'd automatically be logged in without additional steps. However, the act of automatically logging someone in via geolocation has an additional problem: the confused deputy.

Take our last scenario, where a user's device will automatically perform second-factor authentication if it exists within a certain geofence. If our criminal in another country logs in as you during work hours on a weekday, it's highly probable that your geofence for work will automatically accept the login attempt. This is known as the confused-deputy problem because while you aren't logging in, your device is still in the correct location and thus allows the criminal access without your consent.

To work around this problem, additional binding needs to occur to ensure that the device you use to log in has some sort of trust, such as an IP address that matches the location you are expected to log in from. While the confused-deputy problem can be controlled for, it still reduces the effective convenience of geolocation-only authentication security. It's important to realise that a reduction in user 'friction' with authentication almost certainly also reduces the effective security of authentication.

While some two-factor authentication vendors provide geolocation functionality as a small portion of their model, the company Toopher makes this functionality the main feature of their offering. By allowing users to geofence locations after successfully performing two-factor authentication, the next attempt to log in from the same location, as the same user, from the same device, will allow the user to skip additional authentication steps.

As long as the user continues to possess their phone, this authentication process will allow the convenience of single-factor authentication with a second-factor process invisible to the user's awareness.

As geolocation data is likely sent separately from primary credentials, this method would fall into the category of an out-of-band solution. In order for this mechanism to work, however, your device would have to have both global positioning system (GPS) and Internet connectivity to find and transmit geolocation data properly. In large office complexes, underground levels or other situations of limited connectivity, GPS data may be unreliable or inaccurate, or utilise other sources such as Wi-Fi networks to determine a location. Geolocation that is inconsistent can prove to invalidate the gains made by such geo-aware technologies.

For privacy proponents, the collection and storage of geolocation data can be seen as a huge problem. Further, the risk of exposing sensitive details about customers is potentially at stake if an authentication-security vendor was breached and their data pilfered. For many, though, this risk is negligible compared to the dozens of services that likely already compile this data about users.

As the number of geo-aware devices continues to grow, it will be interesting to see how the evolution of mobile computing, geolocation and authentication continue to overlap.

Push-notification-based authentication

Apple and Google have propelled the mobile-device market ahead in just a few short years with iOS and

Android respectively. Among the features offered by these platforms is the concept of push notifications, which are embodied as Apple Push Notification Service (APNS) and Google Cloud Messaging (GCM) in mobile devices of various form factors and purposes.

Push notifications work via a publish/subscribe message model in which a service can instantly transmit small amounts of data to a user's device and then display it for purposes ranging from severe weather alerts to denoting that a new email has just arrived. By appearing on a device's screen in plain view of the user, this mechanism is of great use to prompt a person's immediate action.

In the context of two-factor authentication, push-based notifications enable a technology that typically requires a lengthier process and can streamline those steps to a couple of screen taps. By interacting with a user when an authentication action is required, the typical usage of push notifications can couple neatly with a mobile application to process a request with little effort on the part of the end-user.

While numerous vendors currently offer such technology, Duo Security is best known for their novel innovations surrounding two-factor authentication and push notifications. Through their mobile application, Duo Security's service is able to use a push notification to transmit authentication details to a device, including the requester IP address, their username, the host/service trying to be accessed, a timestamp of the request, and even geolocation data about where the person is authenticating from.

The device itself utilises asymmetric cryptography, wherein the private key is stored within the device and only the public-key portion is sent to Duo Security's service. This allows for the service to verify that the requesting device is authentic in order to prevent fraud. Further, the mobile application will only speak via a cryptographically verified channel back to Duo Security to ensure end-to-end integrity.

The user interface of such a push-based implementation typically allows an authentication request to display the aforementioned details, which can help users identify potential fraudulent logins to their accounts. In some interfaces, including Duo Security's own, a user can simply tap 'Approve' or 'Deny' on the screen and be done with their authentication process. Relative to the somewhat tedious process of typing a code into an application window or answering a phone call and listening for an OTP value, push-based authentication can be extremely quick and easy to use.

Beyond a traditional one-time password generator, mobile applications that are push-notification-aware can be used to display and process additional information that can go beyond a simple authentication request. For example, imagine using your banking website to transfer money from your account to a friend's savings account. Using the same underlying technology as before, details about the transaction – such as how much money you're transferring and into what account those funds are intended to go – can be displayed. In this manner, a user is able to confirm the details about a transaction before deciding to accept or deny it.

While not restricted to push-notification-based mechanisms, transactional verification via mobile devices provides a new level of insight and control for end-users of all types. Whether a system you control is being asked to perform a critical action, or you simply want to confirm a small payment to a friend, the granularity and metadata provided to users give a much better sense of oversight compared to an OTP-based method of authentication.

When a user authenticates to a web service, that session is typically all-powerful for the actions they wish to perform within their role's permissions. This poses a problem when an attacker is able to control the browser's session or host computer. By moving the authentication authority to an out-of-band device and decoupling session-level access from action-level access, services can require additional verification when allowing users to perform a sensitive action.

By leveraging existing technologies like push-notification-based authentication, organisations can give control back to users and take it away from criminals who may be able to trick someone into clicking a link or installing malware. As attackers continue to focus more on individual users rather than on computing infrastructure, the focus must be on moving the role of authentication security from sessions and into more specific actions that have a positive impact on protecting a user's data, finances or privacy.

Biometric authentication factors

Of the factor classes that people interact with, the 'what you are' methods provide for the most sci-fi sense of authentication security we use. Whether by your fingerprint, iris, gait or voice, biometrics can create a signature that can, ideally, match you consistently while protecting against impostors. In sophistication the underlying technologies span a wide range, from easily tricked to military-installation quality.

Unlike other types of two-factor authentication being covered in this book, biometrics don't have a simple 'yes' or 'no' result, but rather a statistical analysis of the input (e.g. fingerprint) and how closely it matches the original sample. Conversely, when you generate a one-time password on HOTP hardware tokens, that value is the only value expected and is guaranteed to work under normal operating conditions. Biometrics work within thresholds of acceptance and those thresholds can cause false positives and false negatives.

Those who have used biometric technology in their professional life likely did so in the context of physical security, such as when entering a secured facility. This process can sometimes be two-factor authentication if a biometric was combined with a PIN to enter at a doorway, for instance. Very few people utilise biometric technology for day-to-day two-factor authentication in the general computing context. One example would be when pharmacists utilise software that requires a password and then their fingerprint to validate that a request actually came from then.

For your average two-factor authentication scenario, biometric-based devices actually make very little sense. They are often clumsy to use, require a larger financial investment in many cases than a simple hardware token, and make people feel uncomfortable about a loss of privacy. While fingerprint scanners have been available for decades in various forms to be used by everyday consumers and businesses, they really never took off in a notable way.

With the release of Apple's iPhone 5S, the previous lack of general biometric adoption changed. Suddenly, millions of everyday consumers were scanning their fingerprints in order to unlock their devices and purchase applications. In addition, concerns over privacy were mostly muted due to the fact that the device stores all fingerprint data required for verification internally, essentially in an irretrievable manner. This lack of data transmission to Apple means that people's privacy can both remain and still benefit from the convenience of this biometric's workflow.

Interestingly, however, Apple's Touch ID technology is becoming effectively focused, in its purest form, on being a factor substitution and not a second factor of authentication. When a user scans their fingerprint, the device will allow them to bypass entering their typical PIN. At this time, users are unable to require both a PIN and a fingerprint scan to unlock the device, which would, of course, provide that two-factor scenario. Third-party developers can still utilise this technology alongside a PIN if they so choose, to provide that experience in applicable contexts for their own customers.

Many technologists will argue that mobile applications and hardware tokens are doomed when it comes to authentication because biometrics will finally take over. This is a somewhat flawed view because biometric usage requires the ability to input biometric data, process it and then pass that verification on to the system you want to authenticate to. This, again, brings up privacy concerns, and requires hardware and very accurate technology that is both highly reliable and great at preventing fraud. As it stands, mobile devices are our most likely widespread means to adopt any and all biometrics, but they will still be focused on self-contained authentication rather than become a means to transmit to a distant system.

When coupled with mobile devices, biometric technologies are actually powerful for a less than obvious reason. As an example, imagine using a hardware token that generates a one-time password. Anyone that picks that device up off of your desk can read the OTP from the screen and then log in as you. However, if your mobile phone required you to scan a fingerprint before the OTP value showed up, this would add a new level of authentication security. By authenticating the user to the device, we gain trust in our second factor that we didn't have before.

User adoption of mobile devices with basic biometric security features from Apple, and many other vendors, provides an interesting new horizon of security where users authenticate to a device and then that device can authenticate a user to a service. This layered approach gives more integrity to a process that, while already good, becomes even better.

For the near future at least, the purpose and application of biometrics for the average technology user will be to verify that they are permitted access to the device that they possess in order to perform tasks. This both strengthens the integrity of the second factor and helps to limit any privacy concerns that users may have – as long as the relevant device was developed with privacy as a focus, as the iPhone 5S was by Apple.

Organisations looking to deploy biometrics for two-factor authentication should likely consider if the benefit of such a technology is worth deflating the privacy concerns that their employees may have about using it. Further, the cost and complexity of a quality biometric technology may be prohibitive except in scenarios like medical or financial contexts, where certain actions may require two factors to be completed before a critical step can be taken. Ultimately, biometric technology will continue to shrink in size, rise in accuracy and become a more regular part of the everyday consumer's life.

Smartcard verification

While the name is rather ambiguous, typical smartcard devices will often be the size of a credit card and contain a chip inside that performs various cryptographic operations. Other popular form factors include USB drives, key fobs and even mobile phones. Depending on their purpose, these cryptographic operations may help to confirm a financial transaction, allow door access or log someone into their desktop computer. Smartcards often implement the ISO/IEC 7816 and ISO/IEC 14443 standards.

The use of smartcards falls into one of two form factors: contact or contactless. The former type requires the smartcard to be inserted into a reader to function. The latter utilises radio waves of various types to perform either active or passive verification. One of the most common examples of passive contactless smartcards is a proximity card that many businesses use for employee access to buildings. The company HID is rather notable for its wide product line of proximity smartcards, developed for this exact purpose.

In business contexts, multiple attempts have been made since the 1990s to get smartcard technology integrated into the typical worker's computing usage. Your average office employee is still not likely to use smartcard technology on a daily basis, but this varies widely based on country and industry. The health-care and financial industries have higher adoption of smartcards due to enhanced security concerns and usability demands. Being able to have a device that's on your person and provides quick privilege to computer workstations can be an important detail in hospitals.

US government usage of smartcards increased dramatically due to Homeland Security Presidential Directive 12 (HSPD-12) in 2004 to create an identity-card standard for government employees. From this action came the personal identity verification (PIV) card and the associated FIPS 201 standard. This is in addition to the common access card (CAC) that has been issued since the early 2000s to Department of Defense employees and the general US military. Efforts for CAC Next Generation (CAC NG) integrate PIV requirements to satisfy HSPD-12.

For consumers, the EMV standard, which provides enhanced payment security for financial cards, is certainly a widely adopted example of smartcard technology. While

EMV is a specific type of smartcard and is not meant to be general-purpose, it's a great way to introduce the general public to this type of technology and could help adoption in other forms. Further, after the rash of point-of-sale malware attacks against large retailers during 2013 and 2014, the EMV standard is being quickly rolled out in the United States, where it had been previously lagging in usage and deployment.

Today, smartcards are likely paired with a PIN to provide quick and secure two-factor authentication to computers, infrastructure and secured facilities, and for authorising a variety of transactions. Many smartcard technologies are actually single-factor, and do not rely on any knowledge-based factor at all. Products such as SafeNet's eToken PRO Smart Card and Yubico's Neo offer smartcard technology that can be integrated as a second factor. In the case of the Yubico Neo, the device is PIV-compliant so that not only average business users can leverage it, but also those in the US government.

Much like hardware tokens performing OTP functions, smartcards in their generic form are still another piece of technology that you have to protect and remember to bring with you. For this reason, organisations that have BYOD policies may start to look towards the future of smartcard technology successfully used by mobile hardware that can be free to use and easy to remember for all relevant business-use cases.

While mobile security technologies are likely to be the way forward for typical businesses when it comes to two-factor authentication, it's important to remember that an individual industry will have its own needs, nuances and existing technology roadmaps to consider before deciding what technology may appear the most exciting at first glance. Further, the use of mobile devices actually allows NFC, Bluetooth Low Energy (BLE), and USB to act as a means to perform smartcard functions natively.

This is not, of course, to say that smartcards the size of credit cards are on their way out. In many ways, the use of smartcards for applications such as financial (via EMV) and door access is likely only going to continue to rise. Further, most PIV and CAC implementations will likely continue to be done primarily through existing vendors fitting this form factor. The benefit of any smartcard use is that it becomes more familiar to the average office worker and consumer, enabling future use to add high-level security coupled with reasonably cost-effective and manageable devices.

CHAPTER 5: STANDARDS AND REGULATIONS

One security control, many boxes checked

It's no secret that many of the information security projects that are initiated by organisations are run in order to achieve compliance with a certain standard or regulation. Whether your company is a large financial organisation, a small online retailer or a medical care facility, there are certain benchmarks that must be met in order to participate adequately in the given industry vertical. This chapter will detail a number of situations across the world where two-factor authentication is part of the everyday reality in many different industries, from the United States to India.

PCI DSS

Assuredly one of the most widely known security standards in the world is the Payment Card Industry's Data Security Standard, better known as PCI DSS. Version 3.0, the most recent revision, was released in November 2013, and went into effect for all PCI-related organisations in January 2015. If your organisation is involved in processing credit cards in any manner, some – or all – of PCI DSS v3.0 likely applies to you.

The PCI Security Standards Council (SSC) comprises five global leaders in payment-card issuance, including Visa Inc., American Express, JCB International, MasterCard and Discover Financial Services. This group ultimately determines what PCI DSS revisions will contain in terms of security guidance to give a baseline for payment-processing organisations to meet. While the challenges for smaller organisations to meet PCI compliance can often be daunting, this standard is seen as a minimum level of security that *most* organisations should meet, not just those handling payments.

Ever since the first release of PCI DSS v1.0, Requirement 8.3 has represented the use of two-factor authentication in the context of remote authentication scenarios, such as VPN usage. Over a decade later, the language has changed slightly, but focus on the requirement is only being refined by the PCI SSC. In fact, Requirement 8.3 was recently split into two verification procedures in v3.0 to put an even finer point on what the PCI Council sees as acceptable compliance.

Unlike PCI DSS v2.0, the v3.0 guidance doesn't simply ask a qualified security assessor (QSA) to observe a single employee logging into a remote-access device to determine that two-factor authentication is deployed. With v3.0, the QSA handling the audit should inspect system/device configurations to determine that two-factor authentication is actually set up and enabled.

While these changes may seem minor, they are a dramatic step in terms of the version-to-version changes that the PCI SSC makes for an existing requirement. This guidance now makes organisations do more than just buy a security solution; rather they must actually configure it for their organisation and enrol users in order to benefit properly from its existence. All too often, security technology is acquired but rarely deployed in a meaningful way. The PCI SSC putting extra emphasis on two-factor authentication is a significant step forward to spur additional adoption.

It should be noted, of course, that after the swath of retail breaches in 2013 and 2014, the PCI SSC is undoubtedly more focused than ever on reducing breaches by pushing for stronger guidance via PCI DSS. With both Target and Home Depot allegedly being breached in part by criminals possessing stolen credentials, it's unlikely that the PCI SSC isn't taking notice of which security controls to continue shoring up guidance for.

Whether an organisation is PCI compliant when a breach occurs is difficult to answer, since most are only checked once a year. It's worth noting, however, that organisations that prevent an attacker's lateral movement through two-factor authentication are surely better off than those that do not.

HIPAA

In the United States, the Department of Health and Human Services (HHS) provides guidance for dealing with sensitive health-care data to protect the privacy of patients. The most notable of this guidance is in the form of the Health Insurance Portability and Accountability Act, otherwise known as HIPAA. In addition to the original Act of 1996, there have been subsequent additional Acts and rules to assure further protection of private health-care data, including electronic protected health information (ePHI).

In 2006, HHS released a 'Security Rule' that covers remote access to ePHI data. In this guidance, it requires the implementation of two-factor authentication, but then provides examples such as using a security question to satisfy this request. Intrepid readers will remember from earlier in this book that what HHS has provided for risk mitigation is actually misleading to those seeking guidance on the problem at hand. Remember, two-factor authentication is achieved through using two different factor classes during an authentication transaction. By recommending that a password and a challenge question be coupled, HHS is actually saying one thing but giving an example of another.

Unfortunately, not even government-approved security guidance is always accurate. Due to this, many health-care entities will use 'challenge questions' and state erroneously that they have indeed utilised two-factor authentication. Had the guidance stated that they should use 'strong authentication', their example would have been an acceptable one. Such missteps in guidance leave many security professionals and general technologists confused at the actual intent of the rule.

With electronic health records (EHR) becoming more a part of our daily lives, the need to provide secure access to health-care information is increasing rapidly. While formal guidance around additional authentication security is somewhat lacking, it would stand to reason that, in the future, HHS would take a stronger position on accessibility of EHR through controls such as two-factor authentication. With so many successful phishing attacks and other means of stealing the credentials of users, betting on the likelihood that EHR data will be safe in the long term is unsafe.

FFIEC

In 2005, the Federal Financial Institutions Examination Council (FFIEC) of the United States released their *Authentication in an Internet Banking Environment* guidance. This original document was later supplemented in 2011 to amend some of the earlier details in order to align it better with modern Internet banking realities. Much like their government counterparts, those at the FFIEC also noted the need for two-factor authentication, but even more ambiguously than did HHS. In their guidance, they refer to "dual customer authorisation through different access devices", which can easily be represented by many methods of two-factor authentication.

One important idea conveyed within this guidance is the premise of out-of-band verification for transactions. In essence, this could involve phone call-back techniques, push notifications or any other traditional two-factor authentication mechanism applied directly to financial transactions. By combining the security of a two-factor solution with transaction-level verification, the end-user gains even more control and granularity over the security of their banking activities on existing mobile banking applications.

While it would seem the FFIEC's guidance has the right intent, much like HHS they've been entirely too unclear as to what the real technical implementation should be in order to achieve each guidance standard. Hopefully, further amendments to the existing guidance or entirely new guidance will be published to take into account the role that Internet banking is playing in the everyday lives of consumers and businesses alike. After all, the threat posed to an average Internet user becomes very real when their financial accounts can be compromised via a single password through trivial criminal attacks.

India

In early 2014, the Royal Bank of India (RBI) released a document titled the *Report of the Technical Committee on Enabling Public Key Infrastructure (PKI) in Payment System Applications*. While this document outlines a number of technical security controls, including adoption by local and foreign financial systems, it states rather specifically that Internet banking should utilise two-factor authentication.

To provide another point of view on this topic, the document spends much time discussing PKI usage of strong authentication as an alternative to two-factor authentication. There are a number of countries, including Sweden, Norway and China, which use PKI for their banking institution's security programs. One reason for this PKI usage is the ability to sign transactions using a person's private key in order to provide integrity to that action. Part of this rationale is the idea of non-repudiation applied to banking transactions.

Non-repudiation is an important information-security – and legal – concept. Effectively, when a person's private key signs a document, transaction, email or file, many courts will uphold that they were, in fact, the agent who actually performed that action. This certainly could be untrue in that many ways to attack a person that could lead to coerced signing, but this action is often quite binding regardless of potential threats to signing parties.

Still, typical two-factor authentication techniques such as one-time passwords via hardware tokens or SMS are discussed in some detail in RBI's document. More than discussion, there are actual insights into two-factor authentication adoption, such as the cost and deployment of hardware tokens or the latency of receiving an OTP via SMS.

It's quite fascinating to look at the progressive, technical detail provided in RBI's guidance in contrast to some of the high-level documents that similar organisations in the United States put out. In India there seems to be a clear and fruitful effort being made to truly add security rather than just checking a box.

Singapore

While India may seem very progressive by pushing hard for two-factor authentication in Internet banking, Singapore makes most countries look bad when it comes to proactive security. In fact, in 2003, Singapore started to recommend that their banks start implementing two-factor authentication, adding firmer guidance to that effect in 2005.

A memo titled *Two-Factor Authentication for Internet Banking* was distributed to all banking CEOs on 25 November 2005, stating that banks were expected to implement two-factor authentication by December 2006. If that wasn't enough, the memo also said that customers should also be required to perform additional authentication for high-risk transactions or actions that impacted sensitive customer data. Comparatively, even as of 2014, you'll find very few banks in the United States that go to those lengths to protect their average banking customer.

Most recently, the Infocomm Development Authority (IDA) of Singapore determined that it would be rolling out two-factor authentication for its SingPass system, which allows citizens to interact with various government services. This action comes on the heels of a July 2014 breach of the service that compromised 1,560 accounts. While that number may seem disconcertingly high, there are actually over 3.3 million SingPass accounts registered as of 2013. The focus on two-factor authentication across Singapore is quite clear, however, and the progressive attitude is certainly a benefit to their citizens.

CHAPTER 6: TWO FACTOR FOR INTERNET END-USERS

Changing the face of two-factor adopters

As has been noted in this book, many of the people who've used two-factor authentication in computing contexts likely did so through their professional careers in a few main industry verticals. Because of this, many of the standards and second-factor technologies we've reviewed are foreign even to a seasoned user of two-factor authentication. Until 2008, the average Internet user was very unlikely to have any access to two-factor authentication for their accounts and thus exposure to these technologies will have been limited or non-existent.

From 2011 to present, there's been a steady increase in the number of online sites and services that provide their end-users the capability to perform two-factor authentication for account security. Interestingly, these efforts to help protect users' accounts permeate online entities of many types, including financial, gaming, social-media, retail and technology providers.

This chapter will present insights from a data set that I created in 2014 while working for two-factor service provider Duo Security. We'll review what's happening that's exposing an entire technological generation to a security control previously limited to only the largest corporations and governments.

Early end-user two-factor authentication

The authentication research that I conducted during mid-2014 reviewed available data for over 140 websites and services, each providing some form of two-factor authentication for their end-users. With data going back as far as 2005, I've been able to glean what I consider to be a few of the main reasons we're now seeing two-factor authentication leave the hands of a few focused industries and broaden out to places most people would never have expected.

From 2005 to 2007, seven of the eight online services that publicly provide two-factor authentication security for customers fell under the financial-services umbrella. Investment accounts, business banking and even Internet transactions (PayPal) led the early charge in providing customers with additional authentication security. Unsurprisingly, these institutions were heavily focused on hardware tokens as the primary means to achieve this goal.

In 2008, the gaming company Blizzard provided their players with the means to protect the ownership of their accounts and related digital goods: two-factor authentication for the Blizzard.net service with a hardware token. For people who don't play computer games, this may seem very odd; however, online gaming can be big business and account contents can yield thousands of dollars in certain digital marketplaces. The same rationale that applies to protecting a checking account with two factors can be applied to online gaming services.

Both Amazon Web Services and MarkMonitor provided customers with two-factor authentication in 2009, with

MarkMonitor leveraging VeriSign's VIP platform, which leveraged not only hardware tokens but also mobile applications. Keep in mind that mobile app stores for Apple's iOS and Google's Android only got started in late 2008. While BlackBerry and other mobile platforms certainly had mobile application capabilities before 2008, the groundswell we've seen in mobile application adoption since is unprecedented.

In total, from 2005 to 2010, some 24 sites and services online were enabling users to protect their accounts with some form of two-factor authentication. And while mobile applications were just starting to reshape how computing technology was used, enhanced authentication security was similarly about to evolve quickly.

Google's impact on driving adoption

The Internet giant Google started to provide what they dubbed 'two-step verification' for their customers in February 2011, leveraging SMS, phone call-back and mobile OTP generation via their free Google Authenticator application. This addition to Google's account security is important not only because of Google's ability to influence and shape technology adoption, but also by leveraging the TOTP and HOTP standards in Google Authenticator.

Ostensibly, Google's interest in two-factor authentication was grounded in enabling their user base, in a versatile, easy and affordable manner, to gain better account security. After all, as Google's expansion from search engine and advertising behemoth broadened into their entire line of Google Apps for business needs, the demand for additional security was certainly becoming a front-and-centre topic. By leveraging multiple mechanisms, adopters of their two-factor authentication were able to do at negligible cost – or completely for free – what would cost US$20 or more per person with many other online services.

As Google Authenticator became known by a broader audience, organisations started to 'do as Google does' and configure their own web services to leverage TOTP and HOTP to give additional security. With the nexus of a free mobile application, open standards and plenty of free code to implement those standards, the addition of two-factor authentication quickly became a no-brainer for many services looking to set their offering apart from the competition with regard to security.

In 2011, of 13 sites to add two-factor authentication functionality, nine were leveraging HOTP or TOTP to do so. In comparison, from 2005 to 2010, of 24 services only two were doing so. In fact, Google Authenticator implemented TOTP about a full year prior to the TOTP RFC being finalised. Before the release of Google's app, many organisations were using proprietary soft-token technology like VeriSign's VIP or telephony options instead.

The confluence of the release of Google Authenticator, the TOTP standard's finalisation and the continued blistering growth of mobile-application adoption all likely helped to fuel the growth of the soft-token era that we currently see enabling end-user authentication. As of August 2014, of 141 sites and services online 74 provide TOTP as a method to perform second-factor authentication. Notable services that provide OATH-compliant OTP generation include Facebook, Buffer, LastPass, GitHub, Tumblr and Evernote.

Two-factor authentication and Bitcoin

While this book has covered many broad reasons for an increase in adoption and deployment of two-factor authentication, a less obvious driver is Bitcoin. The hugely popular crypto-currency that started around 2009 put account security in the mind of every entrepreneur in the space who was trying to capitalise on the excitement and explosive growth of the Bitcoin market. As such, the need for protection of individual user accounts for Bitcoin-related services – especially for exchanges – made two-factor authentication an obvious enhancement.

Nearly every reputable Bitcoin service will provide a means to do two-factor authentication for user-account security as a free, value-added feature. Unsurprisingly, this security is almost always done through TOTP, with an astounding 14 in every 15 Bitcoin sites leveraging the standard. By comparison, the next most popular means to provide two-factor authentication is SMS, with only three sites offering it.

Since Bitcoin exchanges and the like are obviously thinking about keeping overheads low and security high, the ubiquity and 'free' price tag of TOTP make this adoption an obvious one for services. Customers, then, are exposed to technology that they may have never heard of before as Bitcoin reaches far beyond traditional IT people and into a broad set of backgrounds and purposes for investing in Bitcoin. Over just the past few years, this wider net has exposed perhaps millions of people to two-factor authentication for the first time.

The reality of Bitcoin breaches and stolen 'wallets' – the means to store Bitcoin you own – continues to concern users of this Wild West of virtual currency and will assuredly only put more focus on the subject of account security. This space may, in fact, help innovation in the area of two-factor authentication, enabling traditionally slow and cautious financial institutions to attempt deploying the solution. Services that want to gain customer trust will surely be thinking hard about how to make their brand stand out for security versus their never-ending stream of new competition.

Fear, uncertainty and doubt

While retail point-of-sale breaches have certainly been a big news topic since 2013, the online threats being faced are no less concerning to consumers. Authentication security has become a notable topic in recent years, as hacktivist groups such as Anonymous and LulzSec have shown the amount of private data and number of passwords that with little effort can be acquired from large corporations.

Numerous popular online companies have been breached in recent years, including DreamHost, LinkedIn, Dropbox, Evernote, Linode, Buffer and Kickstarter. As a result of each of these breaches, all of the organisations deployed two-factor authentication, not only to help protect customer accounts, but also as a way to show that they care about account security. In fact, Dropbox, Linode and Buffer all enabled second-factor options within a month of announcing that they had been breached. This sort of implementation turnaround should, of course, be lauded, but also speaks to the priority that each saw in the addition of two-factor authentication.

Even without formal breaches, the number of accounts that have been brute-forced, phished or otherwise accessed by criminals seems to know no bounds. In 2013, when the Twitter account of the Associated Press was compromised and falsely reported that the president of the United States had been killed, the Dow Jones industrial average fell 143 points. This sort of real-world impact due to a digital persona's erroneous 'reporting' clearly shows that, no matter the medium, consequences can be felt from what seems an otherwise harmless prank. Hysteria can now be put into the world with the help of an administrative password to a blog or social-media account without the review process of a newspaper or television anchor.

The general malaise of passwords as the 'way forward' to account security seems to be at an all-time high. Password-cracking technologies continue to improve – both in terms of software utilised and computing power's affordability – along with breach data still showing that people select terrible passwords. Most recently, the gigantic breach of Sony Pictures Entertainment led to thousands of passwords being discovered across dozens of stolen files. Sadly, these files were both unencrypted and clearly stored in a manner not fit for typical best practice regarding password security.

As consumers continue to realise just how exposed they are through password-only security, their desire to have organisations provide them with better control of account ownership increases. The website twofactorauth.org provides a list of services that currently provide two-factor authentication for usage by end-users. With both a basic listing of technologies enabled and instructions to configure the feature, this website helps to empower users who may not otherwise know that they have additional security controls to utilise.

Quite often, features are added silently to services and never presented in a meaningful enough way to spur real adoption. For example, if you told even technical users that Facebook has offered two-factor authentication since 2011, they'd look at you askance. Security features are just not always as well publicised, as 'business' features seem to be.

Choice in the marketplace

One final driver behind the current increase in two-factor authentication adoption is simply that many more choices exist today than they did a decade ago. Companies like Duo Security, Authy, Toopher, Clef, LaunchKey, Rublon and WiKID all provide varying levels of feature sets and price points to fit just about every conceivable need out there. With the advent of Cloud computing, the scalability and service model of two-factor authentication have changed dramatically over the course of only a few years, helping to enable more services and users than ever to gain great authentication security.

There's no doubt that well-known companies like RSA, Symantec and VASCO will continue to hold a large portion of the enterprise market share for many years to come, but the number of Cloud service providers out there that need a business-to-business-to-consumer (B2B2C) option is quickly growing. These smaller, broadly used organisations are looking for clever and convenient ways to help their customers gain security without a great deal of overhead or cost. Thus the market space, now with over 40 providers of two-factor authentication, is ripe for innovation, lowering costs and better ease of integration. It's a great time to be a security-centric consumer right now.

It's important to remember that while enterprise and government needs have driven the two-factor authentication space for well over 20 years, the use of computers, the Internet and personal electronics has started to necessitate better security for your average consumer. The spreadsheets we hold in Dropbox, the images we upload to iCloud, and the emails we send from Gmail are all key parts of our personal and professional lives. These days, when accounts are breached, the impact can be catastrophic and the fallout hurtful to our prosperity.

The Fast IDentity Online (FIDO) Alliance has proposed two standards to continue the democratisation of authentication security for end-users of all types. With both their Universal Authentication Framework (UAF) and Universal Second Factor (U2F) protocols, the FIDO Alliance is focused on widening the adoption of sustainable, industry-driven standards around authentication. Further, their partnerships with major corporations will help resulting technologies to improve user authentication beyond just the technical elite.

Not only do FIDO Alliance protocols focus on streamlining the many ways we handle authentication, but they have also improved the overall security provided. For instance, the U2F protocol prevents users from being maliciously tricked into sending an OTP value to an attacker's fraudulent website. By helping protect the user rather than relying solely on their discretion, U2F provides not just a second factor, but also one that compensates for social-engineering techniques used by attackers. With U2F, FIDO has actually considered the user, and is helping them to help themselves. This is real, meaningful progress.

CHAPTER 7: CONCLUSION

Looking forward

As technology continues to evolve with more focus on the individual user, authentication security will only become more exciting and more important. I foresee a time in which the many wearable and mobile devices we possess will become a core aspect of authentication, with many methods used across two or three factor classes, providing for greater authentication intelligence.

It's been said that Google uses over 50 different 'signals' of data to provide filtered search results to its users. In a similar manner, I believe that authentication signals will ultimately be the way that we will provide assurance to prove the digital identities we claim. The various forms of computing device that the average consumer will possess is sure to increase not only in sheer number but, perhaps more importantly, in technical capabilities.

Imagine, for instance, that your smartwatch, mobile phone, laptop computer, tablet, car and smartglasses can all act as sources of 'truth' for your authentication context. By combining personal-area networks (e.g. Bluetooth), local-area networks (e.g. Wi-Fi), wide-area networks (e.g. your Internet connection) and the geolocation data of each device (e.g. your phone's physical location), the intelligence of the network of 'who you are' becomes higher in confidence for the systems you authenticate to.

In the current era, a mobile phone with a private key might act as the basis for a system to believe that your second-factor technology is being possessed by you. Let's take this to the next level with the following plausible layered-authentication example:

1 Require a user to scan their thumb print to accept a push-authentication request.
2 Transmit the geolocation from three devices they have on their person.
3 Execute a challenge-response operation from each device communicating with the others via Bluetooth Low-Energy (BLE).

Suddenly, the level of trust has gone up immensely. We're on the cusp of not only two factors, but perhaps three factors, each with two or three methods utilised, automatically 'accepted' through a quorum of device awareness.

Much like other computing technologies, two-factor authentication can be as simple or as complex as someone wishes it to be. Whether your desire is to protect a blog, a small business or millions of enterprise users, there are two-factor authentication options available to cover your needs. With dozens of ways to perform a second-factor authentication operation, the requirements of any organisation can be met for even the oddest edge cases through a combination of biometric and physical methods.

The Internet of Things

To provide the level of interconnected authentication security I've proposed above, the rapid expansion of the Internet of Things (IoT) will be required to fully realise this vision. With estimates of nearly 5 billion IoT devices through 2015 alone, the mixture of broad deployment and connectivity will provide the requisite communication between disparate devices and technologies needed.

While the potential for IoT to increase authentication security exists, the growth of IoT actually creates a greater need for improved authentication security altogether. Thus we're waiting to see whether we can leverage IoT quickly enough to gain better authentication security before the threats facing IoT security manifest.

When passwords are stolen, they often unlock access to email, financial accounts, health information and other data that people want to protect. Now, consider what is at stake when IoT devices can be compromised over the Internet or through an ill-protected Wi-Fi network. Attackers may be able to set a person's oven to overheat, watch a family through an IP camera or even unlock the front door to someone's home. While data theft is certainly detrimental to a person's life, true physical harm and a vast reduction in personal privacy are at stake within the scope of IoT.

Similar to the growth in two-factor authentication we've seen with computing's expansion, the Internet of Things will likely be the next driver behind the need for improved authentication security. Password-only security doesn't translate well when devices that control parts of our lives can be compromised just because someone chose a poor password or was tricked into giving it to a criminal.

IoT vendors have a chance to put user security first, and to make actors in a growing space consider what is at stake *before* harm befalls users. This reality only becomes clearer when we consider that cars are now becoming Internet-enabled and accessible through smartphone applications. Technology as a whole is reaching a tipping point where movie plotlines begin to look like actual threats to human life. Authentication security has come a long way but needs to continue to improve before we're ready to take on these great threats facing billions of users.

In parting

The subject of two-factor authentication is broad. This book, unfortunately, can only scratch the surface of its breadth due to the wide spectrum of technologies, the dozens of implementation scenarios and the quickening pace of its adoption. We're at a very exciting, revolutionary period of authentication security and the need has never been greater for it. The marketplace is undergoing a renaissance of sorts, with the focus not only on enterprise security, but also on the needs of every consumer, end-user and concerned technology participant.

If this book presented an entirely new subject matter to you, an ideal outcome would be to have you seek out which means you could use to enable two-factor authentication. If you were already familiar with this topic, a favourable outcome would be that you're now looking at the subject with a wider-angle lens and a more comprehensive sense of what the subject encompasses.

With your newfound knowledge, perspectives and insight, go empower your family, friends, co-workers and bosses on the realities of two-factor authentication security. The risks to our security may be many, but so are our means to protect ourselves. Let's make sure that those who would otherwise become victims instead become aware and secure.

REFERENCES

Fred Cohen, "A Short History of Cryptography Introductory Information Protection", 1995, *http://all.net/edu/curr/ip/Chap2-1.html*

Chris Savarese and Brian Hart, "The Caesar Cipher", Historical Cryptography Website, 1999, *http://www.cs.trincoll.edu/~crypto/historical/caesar.html*

Cornelis Robat, "ATM (Automatic Teller Machine)", The History of Computing Project, 17 April, 2006, *http://www.thocp.net/hardware/atm.htm*

Federal Financial Institutions Examination Council, *Supplement to Authentication in an Internet Banking Environment*, 2011, *https://www.ffiec.gov/pdf/Auth-ITS-Final%206-22-11%20(FFIEC%20Formated).pdf*

"About OATH", Initiative for Open Authentication, 2012, *http://www.openauthentication.org/aboutOath*

OATH Members list, Initiative for Open Authentication, 2012, *http://www.openauthentication.org/members*
WiKID Systems, "Key Fobs are an expensive hassle!", *https://www.wikidsystems.com/learn-more/Problem/hardwaretokens*

Brian Krebs, "Sources: Target Investigating Data Breach", Krebs On Security, 18 December 2013,

References

http://krebsonsecurity.com/2013/12/sources-target-investigating-data-breach/

Brian Krebs, "Target Hackers Broke in Via HVAC Company", Krebs On Security, 5 February, 2014, *http://krebsonsecurity.com/2014/02/target-hackers-broke-in-via-hvac-company/*

Google, "Stronger security for your Google Account", *https://www.google.com/landing/2step/*

"Setting Two-Factor Authentication Login Requirements", SalesForce Help & Training, *https://help.salesforce.com/HTViewHelpDoc?id=security_require_two_factor_authentication.htm*

John Leyden, "One in 200 success rate keeps phishing economy ticking over", The Register, 7 December 2009, *http://www.theregister.co.uk/2009/12/07/phishing_hit_rate/*

Mike Lennon, "Dyre Malware Targeting Salesforce User Credentials", Security Week, 8 September 2014, *http://www.securityweek.com/dyre-malware-targeting-salesforce-user-credentials*

"Secure Passwords? Patented One-Time Password Technologies and their Effect on Privacy", University of Portsmouth, 3 December 2007, *http://mosaic.cnfolio.com/M591CW2007C102*

References

Olga Kharif, "EMC Losing Ground as Smartphones Displace RSA Tokens", Bloomberg , 27 March 2013, *http://www.bloomberg.com/news/2013-03-27/emc-losing-ground-as-smartphones-displace-rsa-tokens.html*

Jeff Carpenter, "Did You Know: Trends in RSA SecurID® Two-Factor Authentication", RSA Security, 10 April 2012, *http://russia.emc.com/collateral/rsa/eventpresentations/04-10-12-Two-Factor_Auth.pdf*

M'Raihi, et al, "OCRA: OATH Challenge-Response Algorithm", Internet Engineering Task Force , June 2011, *http://www.ietf.org/rfc/rfc6287.txt*

M'Raihi et al, "HOTP: An HMAC-Based One-Time Password Algorithm", Internet Engineering Task Force, December, 2005, *http://www.ietf.org/rfc/rfc4226.txt*

M'Raihi et al, "TOTP: Time-Based One-Time Password Algorithm", Internet Engineering Task Force, May 2011, *http://www.ietf.org/rfc/rfc6238.txt*

Andrew Y. Lindell, "Time versus Event Based One-Time Passwords", Aladdin Knowledge Systems Ltd., 2007, *http://www3.safenet-inc.com/blog/pdf/time_vs_event_based_otp.pdf*

Archie Cobbs, "How one-time passwords work and how they integrate with HTTP authentication", mod-authn-otp Google Code Repository, 8 July 2009,

References

https://code.google.com/p/mod-authn-otp/wiki/OneTimePasswords

Kevin Cernekee , "stoken - Software Token for Linux/UNIX", SourceForge Wiki, 7 July 2014, *http://sourceforge.net/p/stoken/wiki/Home/*

Mohit Arora, "Understanding the security framework behind RSA SecurID", Embedded, 9 November 2011, *http://www.embedded.com/design/safety-and-security/4230483/Understanding-the-security-framework-behind-RSA-SecurID*

TOTP Token - FortiToken-200/200CD, Fortinet, *http://www.fortinet.com/products/fortitoken/password-tokens.html*

DIGIPASS GO 6, VASCO, *https://www.vasco.com/products/client_products/single_button_digipass/digipass_go6.aspx*

GOLD OTP Authenticator with Challenge Response, SafeNet, *http://www.safenet-inc.com/multi-factor-authentication/authenticators/one-time-password-otp/gold-challenge-response-token/*

DIGIPASS 260, VASCO, *https://www.vasco.com/products/client_products/esignature_digipass/digipass_260.aspx*

OTP c300, FEITIAN, *http://www.ftsafe.com/product/otp/ocra*

References

Lucian Constantin, "Malware hijacks World of Warcraft accounts despite two-factor authentication", Computer World, 7 January 2014, *http://www.computerworld.com/article/2487408/malware-vulnerabilities/malware-hijacks-world-of-warcraft-accounts-despite-two-factor-authentication.html*

Hagrin, "The PayPal Security Key", Hargrin's Blog, 3 March 2007, *http://www.hagrin.com/273/the-paypal-security-key*

PayPal Security Key, PayPal, *https://www.paypal.com/us/cgi-bin?cmd=xpt/Marketing_CommandDriven/securitycenter/PayPalSecurityKey-outside*

IDProve 700 Display Card, Gemalto, *http://www.gemalto.com/Products/otp_display_card/index.html*

Ben Popken, "Paypal's New Security Card Fits Inside Wallet", Consumerist, 2 August 2010, *http://consumerist.com/2010/08/02/paypals-new-key-card-fits-wallet-but-doesnt-regen-every-30/*

DIGIPASS® GO 215 single-button authentication and e-signing, VASCO, *https://www.vasco.com/products/client_products/esignature_digipass/digipass-go-215.aspx*

Lance Whitney, "RSA to replace SecurID tokens following breaches", CNET, 7 June 2011,

References

http://www.cnet.com/news/rsa-to-replace-securid-tokens-following-breaches/

Zeljka Zorz, "RSA admits SecurID tokens have been compromised", Help Net Security, 7 June 2011, *http://www.net-security.org/secworld.php?id=11122*

Yubikey Personalization Tools, Yubico, *https://www.yubico.com/products/services-software/personalization-tools/*

Yubikey Hardware, Yubico, *https://www.yubico.com/products/yubikey-hardware/*

"The World in 2010, ICT Facts and Figures", International Telecommunication Union, 20 October 2010, *http://www.itu.int/ITU-D/ict/material/FactsFigures2010.pdf*

Natasha Lomas, "Gartner: Smartphone Sales Finally Beat Out Dumb Phone Sales Globally In 2013, With 968M Units Sold", TechCrunch, 13 February 2014 *http://techcrunch.com/2014/02/13/smartphones-outsell-dumb-phones-globally/*

Twilio Messaging Pricing, Twilio, *https://www.twilio.com/sms/pricing*

Jon Oberheide, "Early Results from X-Ray: Over 50% of Android Devices are Vulnerable", Duo Security's Blog, 12 September 2012,

References

https://www.duosecurity.com/blog/early-results-from-x-ray-over-50-of-android-devices-are-vulnerable

Michael Mimoso , "Zitmo Trojan Variant Eurograbber Beats Two-Factor Authentication to Steal Millions", Threatpost, 6 December 2012, *http://threatpost.com/zitmo-trojan-variant-eurograbber-beats-two-factor-authentication-steal-millions-120612/77287*

Josh Davis, "Two Factor Auth List", Two Factor Auth, *https://twofactorauth.org/*

Shubham Shah, "How I bypassed 2-Factor-Authentication on Google, Facebook, Yahoo, LinkedIn, and many others", Shubham Shah's Blog, 3 May 2014, *https://shubh.am/how-i-bypassed-2-factor-authentication-on-google-yahoo-linkedin-and-many-others/*

"Confused deputy problem", Wikipedia, 27 June 2014, *http://en.wikipedia.org/wiki/Confused_deputy_problem*

Toopher, *https://www.toopher.com/*

"Assisted GPS", Wikipedia, 24 September 2014, *http://en.wikipedia.org/wiki/Assisted_GPS*

"Apple Push Notification Service", Apple iOS Developer Library, 31 October 2014, *https://developer.apple.com/library/ios/documentation/NetworkingInternet/Conceptual/RemoteNotificationsPG/Chapters/ApplePushService.html*

References

"Android version history", Wikipedia, 11 November 2014, *http://en.wikipedia.org/wiki/Android_version_history*

Chris Hayes, "Push Notifications -- Not Just for Games Anymore", SecureAuth, 29 September 2013, http://www.secureauth.com/blog/push-notifications/

"Multi-factor authentication", Wikipedia, 27 October 2014, *http://en.wikipedia.org/wiki/Multi-factor_authentication*

"Fast and Easy: One-Tap Authentication", Duo Security, *https://www.duosecurity.com/product/user-experience/authentication*

"iPhone 5S Specifications", Apple, *https://www.apple.com/iphone-5s/specs/*

Rich Miller, "Biometrics in Data Centers: Palms or Eyeballs?", Data Center Knowledge, 23 September 2008, *http://www.datacenterknowledge.com/archives/2008/09/23/biometrics-in-data-centers-palms-or-eyeballs/*

"Types of Biometrics", Biometrics Institute, *http://www.biometricsinstitute.org/pages/types-of-biometrics.html*

iPhone 6 Touch ID, Apple, *https://www.apple.com/iphone-6/touch-id/*

References

"The integration of smart card readers into personal computers", Smart Card Alliance, *http://www.smartcardalliance.org/resources/lib/DSI_Reader_Paper.pdf*

"Common Access Card (CAC)", DoD ID Card Reference Center, *http://www.cac.mil/common-access-card/*

"PIV & FIPS 201 Solutions", HID Global Corporation, *http://www.hidglobal.com/government/piv*

Riley Waters, "Cyber Attacks on U.S. Companies in 2014", The Heritage Foundation, 27 October 2014, *http://www.heritage.org/research/reports/2014/10/cyber-attacks-on-us-companies-in-2014*

"A Healthcare CFO's Guide to Smart Card Technology and Applications", Smart Card Alliance, February 2009, *http://www.smartcardalliance.org/resources/lib/Healthcare_CFO_Guide_to_Smart_Cards_FINAL_012809.pdf*

Homeland Security Presidential Directive 12, U.S. Department of Homeland Security, 22 July 2013, *http://www.dhs.gov/homeland-security-presidential-directive-12*

"Federal Information Processing Standard Publication 201", Wikipedia, 29 August 2013, *http://en.wikipedia.org/wiki/FIPS_201*

Stephane Ardiley , "History of the Common Access Card (CAC)", Security Info Watch, 19 March 2012,

References

http://www.securityinfowatch.com/article/10653434/history-of-the-common-access-card-cac

eToken PRO Smart Card   SafeNetm,
http://www.safenet-inc.com/multi-factor-authentication/authenticators/pki-smart-cards/etoken-pro-smart-card-security/

"Smart Card Authentication", Centrify,
http://www.centrify.com/solutions/smart-card-authentication.asp

Ronnie Manning , "Yubico Presents the First Smart Card with User Presence to Combat Super-Spy Malware", Yubico, 25 February 2013,
https://www.yubico.com/press/press-releases/yubico-presents-smart-card-user-presence-combat-super-spy-malware-2/

"PCI Data Security Standard - Requirements and Security Assessment Procedures - Version 3.0", PCI Security Standards Council, November 2013,
https://www.pcisecuritystandards.org/documents/PCI_DSS_v3.pdf

"HIPAA Security Guidance", Department of Health & Human Services, 28 December 2006,
http://www.hhs.gov/ocr/privacy/hipaa/administrative/securityrule/remoteuse.pdf

References

Diego Matute, "Role of Two-Factor Authentication in Regulatory Compliance and Industry Guidelines", LoginTC's Blog, 19 March 2013,
https://www.logintc.com/blog/2013-03-19-role-of-two-factor-authentication-in-regulatory-compliance-and-industry-guidelines.html

Libicki et al, "Influences on the Adoption of Multifactor Authentication", RAND Corporation, 2011,
http://www.rand.org/content/dam/rand/pubs/technical_reports/2011/RAND_TR937.pdf

Thu Pham, "2014 Costs of a Data Breach by Industry", Duo Security's Blog, 1 December 2014,
https://www.duosecurity.com/blog/2014-costs-of-a-data-breach-by-industry

G. Padmanabhan, "Credit/Debit Card transactions-Security Issues and Risk mitigation measures", Reserve Bank of India, 18 February 2009,
http://www.rbi.org.in/scripts/NotificationUser.aspx?Id=4844&Mode=0

Vivian Yeo, "S'pore banks gear up for stronger authentication", ZDNet, 9 May 2006,
http://www.zdnet.com/article/spore-banks-gear-up-for-stronger-authentication/

Isabelle Chan, "Better authentication allays online banking fears", ZDNet, 18 June 2007,
http://www.zdnet.com/article/better-authentication-allays-online-banking-fears-2062020506/

"Understanding Two-Factor Authentication and Transaction Signing", MoneySENSE, 16 June 2014, *http://www.mas.gov.sg/moneysense/understanding-financial-products/investments/consumer-alerts/understanding-two-factor-authentication-and-transaction-signing.aspx*

M V N K Prasad and S Ganesh Kumar, "Authentication factors for Internet banking", Institute for Development and Research in Banking Technology, *http://www.idrbt.ac.in/publications/workingpapers/Working%20Paper%20No.%2011.pdf*

K. T. Jagannathan, "Two-step authentication must for credit cards: RBI", The Hindu, 23 August 2014, *http://www.thehindu.com/business/Industry/twostep-authentication-must-for-credit-cards-rbi/article6345330.ece*

"RBI for two-stage verification for online banking transactions", The Economic Times, 22 April 2014, *http://articles.economictimes.indiatimes.com/2014-04-22/news/49318793_1_cheque-truncation-system-authentication-transactions*

Sharma et al, "Report of the Group on Enabling PKI in Payment System Applications", Reserve Bank of India, January 2014, *http://rbidocs.rbi.org.in/rdocs/PublicationReport/Pdfs/PKI070214FR.pdf*

References

Chua Kim Lee, "Two-Factor Authentication for Internet Banking Monetary Authority of Singapore", 25 November 2005,
http://www.steptoe.com/assets/attachments/1969.pdf

"Singapore to adopt two-factor authentication system in 2015", The Paypers, 1 December 2014,
http://www.thepaypers.com/digital-identity-security-online-fraud/singapore-to-adopt-two-factor-authentication-system-in-2015/757581-26

Kevin Kwang, "Two-factor authentication for SingPass will be opt-in next year", Channel NewsAsia, 27 November 2014,
http://www.channelnewsasia.com/news/singapore/two-factor-authentication/1496870.html

"ESET Secure Authentication - Second factor authentication and compliance", ESET, 6 November 2013,
http://www.eset.com/fileadmin/Images/INT/Docs/Other/ESA/2FA-and-Compliance.pdf

"App Store (iOS) Wikipedia", 1 September 2014,
http://en.wikipedia.org/wiki/App_Store_(iOS)

"Google Play", Wikipedia, 19 November 2014,
http://en.wikipedia.org/wiki/Google_Play

Mark Stanislav, "PasswordsCon 2014: End-User Authentication Security on the Internet", Duo Security's Blog, 14 August 2014,

References

https://www.duosecurity.com/blog/passwordscon-2014-end-user-authentication-security-on-the-internet

"Bitcoin", Wikipedia, 27 November 2014, *http://en.wikipedia.org/wiki/Bitcoin*

"Anonymous (group)", Wikipedia, 26 November 2014, *http://en.wikipedia.org/wiki/Anonymous_(group)*

"LulzSec hacker helps FBI stop over 300 cyber attacks", BBC News, 26 May 2014, *http://www.bbc.com/news/technology-27579765*

Simon Anderson, "Security Update", DreamHost's Blog, 21 January 2012, *http://www.dreamhost.com/dreamscape/2012/01/21/security-update/*

Nicole Perlroth, "Lax Security at LinkedIn Is Laid Bare", The New York Times, 10 June 2012, *http://www.nytimes.com/2012/06/11/technology/linkedin-breach-exposes-light-security-even-at-data-companies.html*

Dara Kerr, "Dropbox confirms it was hacked, offers users help", CNET, 31 July 2012, *http://www.cnet.com/news/dropbox-confirms-it-was-hacked-offers-users-help/*

Dave Engberg, "Security Notice: Service-wide Password Reset", Evernote's Blog, 2 March 2013,

References

http://blog.evernote.com/blog/2013/03/02/security-notice-service-wide-password-reset/

Christopher Aker, "Security incident update", Linode's Blog, 16 April, 2013, *https://blog.linode.com/2013/04/16/security-incident-update/*

Joel Gascoigne, "Buffer security breach has been resolved – here is what you need to know", Buffer App's Blog, 26 October 2013, *https://open.bufferapp.com/buffer-has-been-hacked-here-is-whats-going-on/*

Yancey Strickler, "Important Kickstarter Security Notice", Kickstarter's Blog, 15 February 2014, *https://www.kickstarter.com/blog/important-kickstarter-security-notice*

Robert Rowley, "An Article About Authentication", DreamHost's Blog, 3 July 2012, *https://www.dreamhost.com/dreamscape/2012/07/03/an-article-about-authentication/*

Vicente Silveira, "Protecting your LinkedIn Account with Two-Step Verification", LinkedIn's Blog, 31 May 2013, *http://blog.linkedin.com/2013/05/31/protecting-your-linkedin-account-with-two-step-verification/*

Dan Wheeler, "Another layer of security for your Dropbox account", Dropbox's Blog, 27 August 2012, *https://blog.dropbox.com/2012/08/another-layer-of-security-for-your-dropbox-account/*

References

Seth Hitchings, "Evernote's Three New Security Features", Evernote's Blog, 30 May 2013, *http://blog.evernote.com/blog/2013/05/30/evernotes-three-new-security-features/*

Christopher Aker, "Linode Manager Two-Step Authentication", Linode's Blog, 2 May 2013, *https://blog.linode.com/2013/05/02/linode-manager-two-step-auth/*

Belle Beth Cooper, "Introducing 2 Step Login for Buffer: The safest social media publishing on the web", Buffer App's Blog, 26 November 2013, *https://blog.bufferapp.com/introducing-the-safest-social-media-publishing-on-the-web*

Nitsuh Abebe, "New Security Features: Two-factor authentication and IP history", Kickstarter's Blog, 23 June 2014, *https://www.kickstarter.com/blog/new-security-features-two-factor-authentication-and-ip-history*

Ashley Feinberg, 'Sony Kept Thousands of Passwords in a Folder Named "Password"', Gizmodo, 4 December 2014, *http://gizmodo.com/sony-kept-thousands-of-passwords-in-a-document-marked-1666772286*

"AP Twitter hack causes panic on Wall Street and sends Dow plunging", The Guardian, 23 April 2013, *http://www.theguardian.com/business/2013/apr/23/ap-tweet-hack-wall-street-freefall*

References

Eli Pariser, "Filter Bubble, or How Personalization is Changing the Web", YouTube, 3 June 2010, *https://www.youtube.com/watch?v=fDhsO_q7aYU*

"Gartner Says 4.9 Billion Connected "Things" Will Be in Use in 2015", Gartner, 11 November 2014, *http://www.gartner.com/newsroom/id/2905717*

Dan Goodin, "How mobile app weakness could let hackers track and unlock a Tesla Model S", Ars Technica, 1 April 2014,
http://arstechnica.com/security/2014/04/how-mobile-app-weakness-could-let-hackers-track-and-unlock-a-tesla-model-s/

Specifications Overview FIDO Alliance,
https://fidoalliance.org/specifications

ITG RESOURCES

IT Governance Ltd sources, creates and delivers products and services to meet the real-world, evolving IT governance needs of today's organisations, directors, managers and practitioners.

The ITG website (*www.itgovernance.co.uk*) is the international one-stop-shop for corporate and IT governance information, advice, guidance, books, tools, training and consultancy.

Publishing Services

IT Governance Publishing (ITGP) is the world's leading IT-GRC publishing imprint that is wholly owned by IT Governance Ltd.

With books and tools covering all IT governance, risk and compliance frameworks, we are the publisher of choice for authors and distributors alike, producing unique and practical publications of the highest quality, in the latest formats available, which readers will find invaluable.

www.itgovernancepublishing.co.uk is the website dedicated to ITGP. Other titles published by ITGP that may be of interest include:

- PCI DSS: A Pocket Guide

  www.itgovernance.co.uk/shop/p-1010.aspx

- Web Application Security is a Stack

  www.itgovernance.co.uk/shop/p-1688.aspx

- CyberWar, CyberTerror, CyberCrime

  www.itgovernance.co.uk/shop/p-511.aspx.

We also offer a range of off-the-shelf toolkits that give comprehensive, customisable documents to help users create the specific documentation they need to properly implement a management system or standard. Written by experienced practitioners and based on the latest best practice, ITGP toolkits can save months of work for organisations working towards compliance with a given standard.

To see the full range of toolkits available please visit:

www.itgovernance.co.uk/shop/c-129-toolkits.aspx.

Books and tools published by IT Governance Publishing (ITGP) are available from all business booksellers and the following websites:

www.itgovernance.eu   *www.itgovernanceusa.com*

www.itgovernance.in   *www.itgovernancesa.co.za*

www.itgovernance.asia

Training Services

Technical solutions are essential for the organisation that takes its information security seriously, but technology is only one part of a robust security posture. Best-practice information security requires the triad of people, processes and technology to be addressed. IT Governance's ISO27001

Learning Pathway provides information security training courses from Foundation to Advanced level, with qualifications awarded by IBITGQ.

Many training courses are available in Live Online as well as classroom formats, so delegates can learn and achieve essential career progression from the comfort of their own homes and offices.

Delegates passing the exams associated with our ISO27001 Learning Pathway will gain qualifications from IBITGQ, including CIS F, CIS IA, CIS LI, CIS LA, CIS RM and CIS 2013 UP).

IT Governance is an acknowledged leader in the world of ISO27001 and information security management training. Our practical, hands-on approach is delivered by experienced practitioners, who focus on improving your knowledge, developing your skills, and awarding relevant, industry-recognised certifications. Our fully integrated and structured learning paths accommodate delegates with various levels of knowledge, and our courses can be delivered in a variety of formats to suit all delegates.

For more information about IT Governance's ISO 27001 learning pathway, please see:

www.itgovernance.co.uk/iso27001-information-security-training.aspx.

For information on any of our many other courses, including PCI DSS compliance, business continuity, IT governance, service management and professional certification courses, please see *www.itgovernance.co.uk/training.aspx*.

Professional Services and Consultancy

With the risk – and severity – of cyber attacks continuing to increase at an alarming rate, two-factor authentication is fast becoming an important factor in managing information security. Organisations that want to ensure their information security posture is as robust as possible are advised to follow international best practice.

ISO27001, the international standard for information security management, sets out the requirements of an ISMS, a holistic approach to information security that encompasses people, process, and technology.

Implementing, maintaining and continually improving an ISMS can be a daunting task. Fortunately, IT Governance's consultants offer a comprehensive range of flexible, practical support packages to help organisations of any size, sector or location to implement an ISMS and achieve certification to ISO27001.

We have already helped more than 150 organisations to implement an ISMS, and with project support provided by our consultants, you can implement ISO27001 in your organisation.

At IT Governance we understand that information security is a business issue, not just an IT one. Our consultancy services assist organisations in properly managing their information technology strategies and achieving strategic goals.

For more information on our ISO27001 consultancy service, please see:
www.itgovernance.co.uk/iso27001_consultancy.aspx.

For general information about our other consultancy services, including for ISO20000, ISO22301, Cyber

Essentials, the PCI DSS, Data Protection and more, please see *www.itgovernance.co.uk/consulting.aspx*.

Newsletter

IT governance is one of the hottest topics in business today, not least because it is also the fastest moving.

You can stay up to date with the latest developments across the whole spectrum of IT governance subject matter, including; risk management, information security, ITIL and IT service management, project governance, compliance and so much more, by subscribing to ITG's core publications and topic alert emails.

Simply visit our subscription centre and select your preferences: *www.itgovernance.co.uk/newsletter.aspx*.